WHAT THE CHURCH OF ENGLAND STANDS FOR

WHAT THE CHURCH OF ENGLAND STANDS FOR

A Guide to its Authority in the Twentieth Century

BY

J. W. C. WAND, D.D.

Bishop of London

LONDON
A. R. MOWBRAY & Co. LIMITED
NEW YORK : MOREHOUSE-GORHAM CO.

First published in 1951

PRINTED IN GREAT BRITAIN BY
A. R. MOWBRAY & CO. LIMITED IN THE CITY OF OXFORD
1575

CONTENTS

5

ACKNOWLEDGEMENT

I am very grateful to my friend Canon Hood, the Principal of Pusey House, Oxford, who kindly read my manuscript and made some valuable suggestions.

W. L.

WHAT THE CHURCH OF ENGLAND STANDS FOR

CHAPTER I

INTRODUCTORY

THE demand for security is the most significant feature of modern life. In the material sphere everything possible is being done to establish for the people as a whole, and not merely for any privileged class, political security, economic security, and social security. Everyone wishes to feel amidst all the changes and chances of this mortal life that he is as safe as he can be, and that he has secured a fair measure of safety for his dependants.

No doubt the special reason for this demand to-day is the extremely insecure position in which the world finds itself during our epoch. Two World Wars in one generation and the threat of a third have made people feel that the very foundations of society may be broken up. Naturally they wish to ensure themselves as far as they can against the possibility of catastrophe. It is recognized that we are living in an interim period, an age of specially rapid transition from one stage of civilization to another. 'Happy is the land,' we say, 'that has no history.' We recognize that there are periods when the course of things runs so smoothly that we can hardly perceive any motion at all. These are the great periods of peace and stability, when everything is taken for granted. In others, however, change is so rapid that the river of time seems almost to be approaching a cataract. Such an age is the present. It is a revolutionary period and the revolution is none the less thorough even where it escapes being violent.

I

Change involves doubt. It is when everything appears stable that our ideas are likely to be most fixed. When everything is on the move it is difficult to find a resting place for the mind. Standards appear to be relative. What is accepted to-day is rejected to-morrow, and we find ourselves occupying a still further position the day after.

The present unsettlement in material conditions is accompanied by a considerable mental disturbance. People have to readjust their ideas of direction and even of their immediate goal while they are actually on the march. In such circumstances they need more than ever some reassurance as to their ultimate aims and objects. They require some standard of judgement within themselves by which they can assess what is going on around them, and above all they need some authoritative guidance by which they can direct their lives and conduct.

For such assurance more and more people are looking to religion. They feel instinctively that if the world is on the move, eternity should be able to supply the fixed point. There, if anywhere, can be found the authority by which all doubts can be resolved. Religion is the activity in which humanity claims most definitely to be in touch with the eternal. If religion could speak with the voice of authority it would give them the sense of security they need.

The religion with which the vast majority of our countrymen are in closest contact is Christianity. Christians commonly believe that there is a three-fold authority which they must obey, that of the Bible, of the Church, and of the conscience. On close inspection, however, it is seen that the authority of each one of these depends in some degree upon the others for its full exercise. It is easy enough to recognize how variable a quantity the conscience may be. It requires a good deal of education before it can be a very reliable guide, and it is so individual a thing that the consciences of any two people are never completely in accord. For that reason alone we need to test our conscience repeatedly by the touchstone of the Bible and the Church. With regard to the Bible, we have learnt to say much the same kind of thing in reference to the varied teaching of its different books. To-day more than ever we appreciate the need for careful understanding before we can imbibe its message as a whole.[1] For such understanding we seek guidance from the Church; and it is that guidance with which we are concerned in the present book.

2

That the Church does claim a measure of authority is, of course, inherent in her very creed. Her assertion that she is Catholic and Apostolic means that she claims to be the universal representative of Christ and to hand on to succeeding generations the revelation she has received from Him. Our Lord Himself said to His Apostles, 'What things soever ye shall bind on earth, shall be bound in Heaven, and what things soever ye shall loose on earth shall be loosed in Heaven.' That was a Hebraic way of saying that the arrangements made by the Church for the good of its members were to be

---

[1] I have already dealt with that particular problem in a companion volume to this, published by Messrs. Mowbray under the title of *The Authority of the Scriptures*.

regarded as divinely authoritative. St. Paul went so far as to say that the Church was the Body of Christ, that is to say, the instrument by which His personality expressed itself upon earth. As the Body of Christ the Church was expected to carry on His work. That work was twofold, comprised under the two terms revelation and redemption. In the sphere of revelation the Church continues to make known the knowledge it has received from Christ concerning the Father. In the sphere of redemption it applies His life to those who accept that revelation so that they may be one with Him both here and hereafter.

There is, however, one special factor that makes some people slow to accept this exposition. The difficulty is that, under present conditions, we appear to have not one single Body of Christ, but a number of *disjecta membra*, torn and separated portions of the original organism. It is not at all clear how far any one of them can justly claim the authority that has been given to the Church as a whole.

It would take us too far from the main point of our consideration to discuss at length the differences which unfortunately exist between the various Christian denominations. We are, however, concerned to assert that the Church of England is a part of the great historic Church of Christendom. Its claim to exercise authority will appear throughout this book, and some justification for that claim will be made clear as the argument proceeds.

In the meantime we can at least recognize that those who are members of it have a right to look to the Church of their fathers for definite direction about the really important things of life. That they have always done so, and never wholly in vain, is clear from any reading of history. That they are doing so with increasing insistence is a matter of common knowledge. On a number of occasions lately in the Church Assembly and elsewhere the laity have demanded a succinct statement of what the Church expects from them. The Convocations are at present discussing the terms of such an authoritative definition. In the meantime the Archbishops of Canterbury and York have put out a small card indicating the seven main duties of Church membership.

This will probably be sufficient to meet the charge that the Church of England is indefinite in its teaching. Other Christian denominations sometimes appear to be clearer. That may be either because they are more ready to limit their emphasis to a few sharply distinguished features, or else because they are prepared to make an overwhelming claim to absolute obedience, leaving the details to resolve themselves afterwards. The Free churches and the churches of the Roman obedience provide us with examples of the two opposite tendencies.

Methodists for instance are very clear about drink and gambling, taking so strong a line against both as almost to make them appear to be the two great commandments of the law. In the Anglican Church teetotalism has never taken the position of a commandment, and, while we have struggled against the evil effects of gambling, we have never yet been able to declare officially that the incorporation of chance into our means of entertainment in itself partakes of the nature of sin. On the other hand it is often said that the Roman Catholic Church claims an absolute authority over every detail of the life of its members. Whether that be so or not, it does claim to give infallible direction in matters of faith. The Anglican Church, on the other hand, claims no infallible authority, and it is notorious that even in matters of worship it allows a wide range of differences. It may therefore appear that there is more room for individual freedom and less emphasis on central authority in the Anglican Communion than in some other parts of Christendom. The question is how far such freedom is compatible with clear and authoritative direction.

It is obvious that some explication of authority is necessary. If we claim that the Church is the guardian of truth and the channel of grace we must try to understand what part the Anglican Communion believes itself to play in both these respects. Others may appear to give the quality of absoluteness to the voice of authority speaking in the 'here and now.' They need not delve into the past or peer into the future. Cardinal Manning said that the appeal to history is heresy. But the Anglican is wedded to history. He can accept no theory of authority which is not already to be found in his foundation documents. He is the heir of the centuries, and he must look into the past to see what is the nature of his Church's authority, how it is based and what is its content.

The purpose of this book is to consider this question.

3

It is a limited purpose, but nevertheless an important one. Many young people, to say nothing of their elders, are asking what is the Church's answer to the problems of the day. We are not proposing to answer that query, but rather to consider the prior question, namely, what right has the Church of England to give any answer at all? Only then may we deal with the spheres in which an authoritative answer can properly be given.

Obviously there are many questions of the day which lie outside the Church's province altogether, and in regard to which the oft repeated demand for an answer from the Church borders upon the absurd. There are, however, at least three spheres in which an answer may be properly expected, namely those of faith, worship, and moral conduct. We shall therefore have to consider not only the Church of England's right to give an answer, but also the nature and extent of her authority in each of these three spheres.

In doing this we shall endeavour to show what directions, in point of fact, the Church does give in these closely related fields. It is believed that as a result of such an inquiry the guidance offered will be found much more clear and direct than is sometimes imagined. The Churchman who knows and uses his Prayer Book, following its instructions faithfully, is not left to face the issues of life without a guide. With its help Church, Bible, and Conscience, all alike under the influence of the Holy Spirit, will give him that moral security which is all that he needs and all that he has a right to ask. He will be shown a practical philosophy, an attitude to life, a vital faith which will enable him to answer his most important problems for himself. And that is the end at which all truly religious authority is aimed.

CHAPTER II

THE CLAIM OF THE CHURCH OF ENGLAND

I

THE desire for authoritative guidance is a completely natural and proper one. Everyone desires to have some guide, philosopher, and friend whom he can trust and to whom he can go in any time of difficulty or doubt. It would be almost incredible that God should leave us without such guidance in the most important decisions of life. Indeed, the whole Christian religion rests upon the belief that God has not left Himself without witness, but that He has revealed both His nature and His will.

There are indeed those who believe that they can get that guidance with sufficient clarity direct from God. As we shall see, there is a real truth in this view. But some go further and profess to believe that there can be and should be no intermediary between God and the individual soul. Direct intuition is all that they need.

> God has some of us whom He whispers in the ear.
> The rest may reason and welcome.
> 'Tis we musicians know.

Such people are accustomed to instance for their classical example the Hebrew prophets who were always able to say, 'God spake unto me saying . . .' They had no doubt that God whispered them in the ear, and they were consequently prepared to stand by their own private conviction against all opposition.

There is no need to deny that there are geniuses in the sphere of religion as in every other sphere. There are especially gifted individuals who pierce to the heart of reality, in goodness, truth, and beauty, with a certainty and an immediacy that leaves everyone else gasping. It would, however, be grotesquely wrong to conclude from this special phenomenon that the genius in any department of life is completely independent of his environment. In fact it would be possible to argue that the genius is to a large extent the product of his environment. The great musician generally springs from musical people; the great writer appears in a notable literary epoch; the man who is capable of the strongest and most independent action has probably acquired his strength of character as a result of contact with others who were quite capable of a certain measure of independence in their own sphere and imparted some of their strength to him.

In any case it is recognized to-day that the Hebrew prophets cannot be considered in isolation. They certainly did a great deal to correct wrong tendencies in the religion of their people, but they were quite definitely inside the national religion and not independent of it. They can no more be dissociated from the Jewish church than the Indian fakir from the Hinduism which forms his natural background. Certainly the Hebrew prophets did not themselves claim, except in rare instances, to be innovators; they claimed normally to be recalling their people to the basic essentials of the national religion. It was the general public and not they who were tempted to stray into by-paths and to depart from the religion that had been once for all revealed to their people.

Thus the main responsibility for the guidance of the Jewish people was always that of the Jewish church, to which the prophets themselves belonged. It was to it

B

that the promises had been made, and it was the church that was expected to preserve the deposit of faith. The hope was that all God's people might turn out to be prophets, not in the sense that they could presume to despise the national religion, but that while faithfully practising the law of their fathers, they would find in it fresh echoes of the Voice of God and would therefore possess that clarity of insight into the true nature of reality, and of the future, which characterized the great prophets.

2

The Church of England claims, as part of the whole Christian Church, to be in the position once occupied by the Jewish church. In this country it is as responsible for the spiritual guidance of the nation as was the Jewish church of ancient Israel. It does not deny for a moment that it may sometimes fall short of its purpose, or that its own vision may become dim. At such times there may be indeed some great leader of thought who will arise to make the old common truth shine with a new uncommon lustre. But, generally speaking, it is the whole authoritative body in which has been renewed the mandate from God and whose duty it is to fulfil His mission to His people. The Church claims, in other words, to be God's trustee in the sphere of religion.

The basis of this authority is not to be found in the fact of 'Establishment.' There is no doubt considerable truth in the contention that the Church's national character gives it a certain prestige in the eyes of the people, and a certain responsibility for the whole nation. There have indeed been times when the Church in this country was as nearly coterminous with the population as was the Jewish church with the Jewish nation. Even when it

became clear that Church and people were not completely identical, it was still possible for the Church to
identify itself with the state and actually to claim state
authority for many of its acts.

Still to-day the Church of England has in some respects
a privileged position. As 'by law established' it is the
official representative of religion in England. It is true
that modern governments do everything possible to
exhibit complete impartiality in respect of the various
denominations, and the Church of England neither expects
nor receives material favour. At the same time when
official acts or ceremonies are consecrated by prayer it is
the Church of England that is called upon to serve in
the ministerial capacity. This inevitably adds a modern
sanction to its already great historical prestige, and
impresses upon it a peculiar measure of responsibility.
In spite, however, of all this it remains true that the basis
of its authority does not lie and has never lain in the state
connection.

Newman, in the first of his famous tracts, asserted
roundly that the guarantee of the Church's authority
was to be found in the Apostolic Succession of its ministry.
This was a valuable and much needed reminder that the
Church is a spiritual society, and that it derives its
authority from spiritual sources. Perhaps nothing could at
the time have more vividly asserted the purely religious
character of the Church's claim.

We must be careful, however, to interpret Newman's
assertion accurately. The Apostolic Succession was not,
and could not be, the sole foundation of the Church's
authority. At best it could only be a guarantee of the
historical continuity of the society and therefore of its
character as part of the original Church. In the last
resort the Church of England can only derive its authority

from the same source from which the Church has always derived it, namely from God Himself. The Church is God's 'Established' Church called out by God Himself from among the nation to perform for the nation the function He has assigned to it.

3

The method employed by God in conferring His authority has always been that of selection. He chose Abraham and made a special agreement or covenant with him, promising that He would use him as a medium of blessing to many generations. This covenant relationship was inherited by Abraham's descendants, and was never entirely lost by them, even in the days when the majority of the nation had proved forgetful, and had wandered after strange gods, and had failed to proclaim the truth it had received to the Gentiles. At such times, so the prophets taught, there still remained the faithful remnant, the 'stock' as they called it of the original tree, from which fresh branches could be expected to grow, and which God could still use as the instrument of His purposes.

The working out of this principle was seen in the life of Christ. He was a prophet in word and deed, but He did not dissociate Himself from the Church into which as a child He had been initiated. He would cleanse it and reform it, but He was very far from regarding it as unnecessary. An illuminating paragraph in Rawlinson's *Authority and Freedom* gives an accurate analysis of the situation:

The attitude of Jesus towards the Church and towards Church institutions was that of a Prophet: that is to say, He took them for granted, but they were not His primary concern. 'The scribes and Pharisees sit in Moses' seat.' The Law is 'the commandment of God,' though the oral accretions of tradition are but precepts of men. The Temple is holy in His eyes: it is His Father's House: He cleanses it with indignation against those who polluted its sanctity. He keeps the Feasts. He goes up to Jerusalem for the Passover. He attends Synagogue on the Sabbath days. He bids the healed leper go and offer the proper sacrifices prescribed by the Law. In a word, the institutional system of Judaism is from first to last the natural background and setting of the personal religion of Jesus. He does not disapprove of religious symbolism, or go out of His way to rebuke superstition. He takes part in a national movement of Repentance, and is baptised with the Baptism of John; and the outward rite mediates to Him a great inward and spiritual experience. It makes Him certain of His mission. It mediates His Messianic Anointing with the Holy Spirit and with power. The Lord is neither an institutional iconoclast nor a Puritan.

When Jesus set about His work, He did it in precisely the same way as His Father had done. He employed the principle of selection. He called out a body of disciples. With them He made a new agreement, a new covenant which He proclaimed formally at the Last Supper, and when the bulk of the nation rejected Him these elect souls became the remnant from which a New Israel sprang.

Thus Jesus was not only conscious of the Church life around Him and of the reform movement within it. He gave a special direction to the reform. He even went so far as to speak of His own 'Church', assembly or ecclesia, 'Upon this rock I will build my church'. He expected it to serve as the nucleus of a new life within Israel, the faithful remnant, the genuine stock. This seems to have been fully recognized by the Apostles whom He had chosen. Their very first concern is to see that their own ranks are complete. They exercise an obvious authority among the steadily growing number of converts, and they use their authority to maintain unity among the scattered congregations. Just as the Jewish church had its Great Sanhedrin, which kept in touch with the Jews dispersed throughout the world, so the Apostolic college at Jerusalem seems to have recognized that its business was to maintain contact with the Christian congregations. Indeed, unity and authority are two of the notes most conspicuously struck in the early Christian documents. In Acts xv we have an elaborate account of what is sometimes called the first Christian Council, in order to show us how these principles worked in practice.

Everyone is aware of the stress laid upon the two principles of unity and authority in the Catholic Church as it emerged from the Apostolic Age. It is true that there were some dissentients, and later from time to time some section of Christian people broke off to found a separate community of its own. There were indeed occasions, as during the Donatists' time in North Africa, when the new sect seemed likely to become larger than the parent body. Normally, however, the sects were comparatively small and the authority of the Great Church was ultimately sufficient to rally adherents and to restore the unity of the common life. To this there was an exception. In the middle of the eleventh century there was a disastrous split between east and west. This was all the less excusable because it was engineered largely for political motives. The essential life of the two bodies retained the same general characteristics, but henceforth there were two representatives of the Great Church each disowning the other.

It was not until the sixteenth century that there came serious divisions which broke up not only the organization of the Church, but also its manner of life. The Reformation produced a number of new bodies which reacted violently against the mediæval church, and endeavoured to reconstruct ecclesiastical polity on what they believed to be a purely Biblical basis. This wholesale rejection of intervening history resulted in a multiplication of sects, for they could arrive at no common interpretation of the Bible. Such a process did, of course, involve the weakening of authority. The new societies cared so little for it that there were repeated splits, although each of them exercised a severe discipline within its own borders. The resultant effect was the utter fragmentation of both political and ecclesiastical unity.

This was the picture presented on the continent of Europe. In England the Reformation took a somewhat different course. There was, it is true, a definite split from the Western Church as represented by the Catholicism centred in Rome, but so far from disowning the intervening centuries of mediæval history, the Church of England claimed that it had maintained unimpaired its continuity with the past. Not only had it kept the creeds of the early Church and a liturgy which embodied the most ancient services, but it claimed that its ministry could show a continuity of succession right back to the Apostolic Age, and it was even prepared to adapt the mediæval canon law to its own needs and circumstances. In fact it asserted that it was still the same Church that it had always been, only without certain abuses that had marred its recent past.

4

Out of the confusion of the Reformation period one fact emerged quite clearly. On the continent of Europe the age-long unitary presentation of Christianity had divided into two separate and opposed forms. On the one side was the ancient Catholic Church, with certain of its characteristics hardened and exaggerated by the Council of Trent. On the other side were the Protestant churches, differing in various respects from each other, but showing the same general opposition to the Roman presentment of Christian faith and practice. Thus Christianity on the continent, instead of appearing in one single guise, now bore two very different aspects. The one side was a closely-knit organism, the other laid the emphasis mainly upon the individual.[1] The former inevitably attached importance to organization and fixed forms, while the other laid far more stress upon inner life and spontaneity. To many it appeared to be the same contrast between law and freedom which occupied so large a part in the consideration of St. Paul. To others it appeared to be a revival of his old conflict between order and antinomianism. While the Catholic Church still taught justification by grace, the new churches insisted upon justification by faith alone. Grace came through the Church: faith was the attitude of the individual. In the last resort that might be represented as the contradiction between collective security and private judgement. It was evidenced in the contrast between the Catholic emphasis on the sacraments and the Evangelical emphasis on belief. Behind this whole range of opposed views and practices there was a very deep-lying difference as to whether man's contact with God is ontological or psychological. Can man really become a 'partaker of the Divine nature,' or must he be condemned to retain his utter separateness while simply drawing up his own will in line with the Will of God?

Obviously there are many considerations which would serve to blunt the sharp edge of opposition between these two contrasted schools of thought. It is not really a case

---

[1] What follows would require some qualification if one had the opportunity to compare and contrast the various policies of Luther, Calvin and Zwingli. As a mere generalization, however, I think the above will stand.

of stark black and white: many shades of grey could be called in to ease the apparent contradiction. In Europe, however, the contrast was very strongly felt and was driven to extremes by both sides with remorseless logic. The result has been to set up rival claims which appear to be completely irreconcilable and to present to the world an appearance of disunity which has gone very far to weaken the authority of Christianity in every sphere.

5

The Anglican position was, and is, an attempt to reconcile these two different schools of thought. The Church of England refused to be impaled on either horn of the dilemma. On the one hand it claims continuity with the whole Church of the past and takes pride in its Catholic tradition. This is not confined to its claim to the Apostolic Succession, but is seen in its use of the historic services of the great Church, its emphasis upon the Sacraments, and its anxiety to build up a proper system of law and to exercise the ancient discipline. On the other hand it has some very close affinities with the Evangelical presentation of Christianity. Like the churches that owe their origin to the Reformation, it rejects the jurisdiction of the Papacy, and it has been among the foremost in the pursuit of Biblical and historical research. In spite of various Acts of Uniformity it has also joined in the protest against over-emphasis upon form and organization, and has insisted upon the importance of a truly spiritual faith.

It cannot be too carefully noted that this is not some modern explanation of Anglicanism arrived at after much participation in present-day debates. It is the original Anglicanism that emerged from the upheavals of the Reformation period. It is the position explained and defended by the great theologians of the sixteenth and seventeenth centuries. Its twin platforms were loyalty to the historic past and faithfulness to Biblical truth. It gladly accepted the New Learning, but it believed that if this revealed the hollowness of some of the Papal claims it enhanced the authority of the ancient Catholic Church. And of that Church it was proud to proclaim itself a part.

In other words, Anglicans do not believe that the two types, Catholic and Evangelical, are irreconcilable. They believe that they are two aspects of the same fundamental Christianity, two sides of the same shield. They believe that both elements can be found in the early leaders of Christian thought, such as St. Augustine and St. Paul, and that the beginnings of both can be traced already in the Gospels and in the teaching of Jesus.

Obviously the endeavour to remain true to the whole of the Christian heritage, and not to emphasize one element at the expense of another, does prevent the Church of England from showing quite so simple a front as is possible for other Christian bodies whose presentation is, in its opinion, more partial. It is often said that Anglicans are really trying to hold together two different religions, and it is sometimes asked how one can expect a Church to show an adequate measure of authority when it speaks with two voices. This dubiety is seen most graphically when different congregations within the Church of England stress different sides of the one teaching. To put the difficulty at its most concrete: all its churches alike in their services have Mattins and Holy Communion, but some emphasize the first as the principal morning service and others the second. This is alleged to be disconcerting to the visitor who may wander from one church to the other not knowing which service he may find, and is often used as an illustration of the lack of unity to be found within the Church of England.

6

This is the situation with which we have to deal in this book. We shall claim that fundamentally Christianity is a life, not simply a creed or a code of morals or a mode of worship, or even a way of living, although it includes all these things. Essentially it is a life, and that life is the life of Christ. Christianity teaches that that life of Christ can be imparted to man, and indeed must be imparted to man if he is to enjoy eternal salvation. This truth has been revealed to us by God Himself through Christ. In Him God has both revealed Himself to man and entered into the life of man. God is no absent landlord of the universe. He permeates the world which He has made, and both reveals Himself to men and makes those who believe in Him partakers of His own nature.

This He does by the ministrations of the Church which He has called out from the world by His own age-long method of selection. To it He gave a fresh start in Christ, who made it His own Body, the instrument by which His own personality can express itself in the world. That universal Church, once so obvious a unity, still exists and performs its authoritative task even although it is now so seriously divided.

One part of that universal Church is the Church of England which is the divinely authorized organization of Christ in this land. Inasmuch as the country is divided into different areas, in each of which an official representative of the Church is placed, it should never be necessary for any inquirer to feel himself far from the guidance that he needs. Each rector or vicar is the accredited agent of the Church in every parish. We may not take to the man, but we can at least appreciate his office. If he is not a person of many parts, and even if he is not personally sympathetic to ourselves, we know that, so long as he performs his allotted task and uses the means that are put into his hand, he is the channel by which the authorized grace of the Church and its authoritative teaching are made available to us. We may indeed reject teaching which he himself is not authorized to give, but so long as he himself is acting under authority we can be assured that he brings us the help God intends us to have.

Long ago a centurion speaking to our Lord revealed that he had discerned the true secret of the Master's capacity to command. 'I also,' he said in effect, 'am a man *under* authority, and for that reason I can give orders to the men under me and expect to be obeyed.' He saw that the source of Jesus' authority lay in His obedience to God. As Christ obeyed the Father, so the Church endeavours to obey Christ. We all live within one authoritative system, and it is only as we are faithful to Him from whom we have received our revelation that we can expect similar faithfulness from those who have received it through us. That is the real secret of authority. We believe that the Church of England is acting under the authority of God, and that therefore she can speak with the voice of authority to her children.

CHAPTER III

THE NATURE OF AUTHORITY

I

IT is important that we should recognize the kind of authority we have in view. There are, of course, many types of authority. There is that of the officer in the army, and there is that of the magistrate on the bench. It can be safely said that neither of these is, strictly speaking, a religious authority at all, although they may be reckoned under that head in so far as it is a religious duty to recognize all duly constituted authority. The centurion's comparison of himself with Jesus applied only to the recognition of authority as such and not to its specific type or context.

It is not denied that from time to time legal and military types of authority have been invoked on behalf of the Church, or that they have been exercised in the sphere of religion on behalf of the State. It is well known that the Roman Empire, tolerant as it normally was in religious matters, endeavoured to force its subjects to accept the Cæsar-worship which was in effect the only form of State religion. It was the Church's refusal to accept this kind of dictation that led to persecution by the State at intervals during the first three centuries. Again, when Christianity had conquered the Empire and had itself become the State religion, it carried the same principle into practice on its own behalf and exercised coercion through the State on both heretics and pagans. This evil principle it followed on occasion in later history, both before and after the Reformation.

Normally it was the State which for logical reasons was anxious to make all its subjects embrace the same cult. Religion was so fundamental an interest of mankind that a serious cleavage in that respect would make political unity almost impossible. Thus in the early Saxon kingdoms when the king was baptized it was taken as a matter of course that his subjects would be baptized also. Throughout the Middle Ages a semblance of unity was preserved, very largely because religion and politics were complementary aspects of the common life. The Church and the Empire were two sides of the same shield. To have broken one would have been to break the whole. Even when at the Reformation that unity was broken, and the separate nations emerged, it was still expected that the various kingdoms would each preserve within itself a twofold unity after the old pattern. Each would follow the religion of the ruler: and the maxim, *cujus regio ejus religio*, was regarded as axiomatic.

In view of such a history it was hardly to be expected that people would easily recognize the true nature of religious authority. The authority of Church and State might seem identical. To-day, however, when it is normal to tolerate many different religions or variations of the same religion in one State, it should be easy to recognize that the authority actually claimed by religion is not that of the State, nor is it of the same nature as State authority. It is not that of a nicely articulated code with legal penalties. It is an authority which must be compatible with individual freedom of choice, recognizing the paramount claim of God.

2

This, of course, takes us back to the Gospels and the teaching of Jesus. 'He taught as one having authority.' 'All authority is given unto me.' 'Ye shall know the truth and the truth shall make you free.' 'Take my yoke upon you and learn of me.' 'My yoke is easy and my burden is light.' 'The Spirit shall guide you into all truth.' Freedom is an even more fundamental postulate of the Gospel than is authority, but true freedom can only come as one submits to the claim of Christ.

This was the main plank in the platform of St. Paul. No one in the whole history of religion has contended more strongly than he for the principle of freedom. He carried the argument right into the psychological depths of human nature. He would not allow his Gentile converts to owe any allegiance to the Jewish law. He drew the strongest possible contrast between law and faith, and if he found any of his converts showing any tendency towards submission to the Law, he would accuse them roundly of rejecting the liberty with which Christ had made them free.

The reason for St. Paul's attitude was twofold. The first was that law engendered pride. If you accept the authority of a legal code your whole effort will be spent in the endeavour to obey it, and if you succeed in obeying it, you will think that you have escaped its penalties by your own merits. Salvation, however, is not something that you can earn; it is something that you can only accept as a free gift. Christ has earned it for you. He offers it to you on the mere condition of your acceptance. That requires complete humility on your part. Into the vacancy formed by that humility He can pour the full riches of His grace. The least motion of pride closes the gap and presents a barrier to the inflow of His Spirit.

The second reason was that only freedom could confer moral character upon any act. Actions performed at the dictation of a law are not, strictly speaking, moral actions at all. They are the responses of an automaton. They are like the gestures of a puppet; authority pulls the strings, the figure responds, but there is no moral value in the response. Or, to put it another way, the sanctions of the law are compulsive: you have no choice but to obey and if you do not obey you die. St. Paul had not been able to obey, and he had died a psychological death.

A moment's reflection shows that there is a certain tension between these two reasons. That tension was not always completely resolved even by those who wished to follow most closely the teaching of St. Paul. Utter humility would lead one to cast oneself completely upon the authority and power of God. It was, perhaps, the most devout soul that found it most easy to think of itself as nothing while God was all. Thus in trying to escape pride it might itself become a puppet, not of the Law but of God. Even so great a psychologist as St. Augustine did not always escape this difficulty. His famous saying, '*Da quod jubes et jube quod vis,*' 'Give what Thou command-est and command what Thou wilt,' did come dangerously near making the soul an automaton, under the complete control of an all-powerful Deity. Yet it may be said that this difficulty was theoretical rather than practical. In actual fact the Christian soul, the more definitely Christian it was, always knew the possibility of choice either to accept or to refuse the motions of God's grace. It has probably never found itself greatly disturbed by the paradox of yielding itself as a slave into the hands of a God whose service is perfect freedom.

This takes us back once again to the heart of the Gospel and to the example of Christ.

It is well known that Jesus Himself would not compel any man's belief, much less his obedience. In the famous account of the Temptation in the wilderness, the Devil is said to have taken our Lord to the pinnacle of the temple and to have invited Him to cast Himself down from it in reliance upon the protective power of His Father. If He had been supported in mid-air by the hands of angels and returned safely to the pinnacle from which He had cast Himself, or if He had been lowered unharmed to the ground, a notable miracle would have been performed. Such a portent would have compelled belief on the part of all beholders. By refusing this temptation our Lord chose the hard way of commending Himself to every man's conscience in the sight of God. It was a reasoned and willing response that He desired, not the submission of a mind bludgeoned into belief.

3

Truly religious authority can be described as paternal or pedagogic. It is like the authority of a parent or a teacher.

To mention these two analogies not only explains the character of religious authority but shows its necessity. No child can be brought up without authority. It may have to learn to obey long before it understands the reason why. It may have to be told not to sit on the wet grass, and it may not understand the warning of the possible consequences of disobedience in the way of a rheumatic chill, but it will still be expected to obey. At the same time the wise parent will, as far as possible, teach it the reason, even while enforcing the command. Similarly all teaching is done at first on the basis of

c

authority. A child has to learn the rules of mathematics or grammar. Only as it learns to apply them will it understand the reason for them. It is probably not until they get to the university that most men acquire the habit of digging into the roots of every authority to find out its reason. Only then do they come to the position of being able to say, 'Now we believe not because of thy words, but our own eyes have seen.'

It is of the nature of such authority, paradoxical as it may seem, to be trying always to make itself unnecessary. It will be training those subjected to it to exercise a competent judgement of their own. Only so can the treasured wisdom of the ages be handed on to each succeeding generation and be enlarged in its passage. If there is no freedom, there will be no improvement in the tradition; and if there is no tradition, each generation will start at the same point as did its predecessor. It follows that the kind of authority of which we speak does not claim to be infallible. If it were infallible there could be no freedom. Any kind of inquiry would be out of place, and would indeed be insulting. There is a good deal to be said for Bishop Butler's dictum that 'probability is the guide of life.' We may often feel that there is something like a moral certainty, but that is very far from a mathematical certainty. The latter is demonstrable, the former is not. The latter compels acceptance unless we wish to be ranked as mentally defective: the other demands the response of faith. We have to stake our future upon it. That is a moral effort, an effort which is proper to us as human beings. Warburton said that the authority of the Church of England was 'competent but not infallible.' That in the last resort is the only kind of authority for which a religious person ought to ask.

4

We have already suggested in a previous chapter that the kind of authority offered us is to be found in three different sources, the Bible, the Church, and our own conscience. It is worth while examining this threefold cord, upon which indeed our spiritual safety depends, a little more closely.

The Bible is the Word of God. It not only records the history of revelation, but it actually gives us the revelation as God has vouchsafed it. We are not to expect the revelation to be expressed with equal clarity and force in each and every part of the Scriptures. We do indeed take the Bible as a whole, but it is composed of various volumes. It shows God more and more clearly revealed in many parts and in diverse manners until the complete revelation comes in His Son. In the later books this final revelation is examined and its consequences analysed by Jesus' more immediate followers.

It must be remembered that the purpose of the Bible is not to teach us science, geography, or history, but to make us familiar with a Person. In it God speaks to us, and we are expected to learn to know God, as we get to know our friends, through His conversation. It is true, of course, that God is revealed to us also through His acts, but the acts are themselves 'words' of God, means of His self-expression. This is sometimes forgotten by those who rely upon isolated texts of the Bible. The Devil, we are told, can quote Scripture for his purposes. What we need is to know the whole Bible in such a way that we can discern God speaking through it all, and so arrive at His full self-revealing. We have here all doctrine that is necessary for salvation. The Church of England teaches that no doctrine may be maintained as necessary to salvation that cannot be derived from the Scriptures. But we have always to remember that our salvation is effected through our relations with Christ. The doctrine must never be allowed to get between us and the Person. It should be a guide to Him. Christianity, as we have already said, is a life, the life of God mediated through Christ. What is necessary above everything is that we should have immediate contact with Him. The Bible, as His Word, gives to the believer immediate contact with the God who speaks.

5

The second thread in this threefold cord is the Church. The Church is the repository of the revelation. It was the Church, whether Jewish or Christian, which actually produced the Bible. Its members wrote the volumes, its councils authorized their use, and compiled the final book. These are not the traditions of men acting against the Spirit of God. The Spirit of God guides the Church as He guided the writers. Because the Church is composed of fallible men we must recognize that they may make mistakes. Yet we believe that the divine purpose has been served throughout, and that the Spirit of God is at work in the Church over-ruling their mistakes. Just as in the Bible God could pursue His spiritual purpose even through the fallible history and science of the various periods in which the books were written, so He has guided the Church in the compilation of the Bible and in drawing essential doctrines from it.

What the Church has done is to summarize the spiritual teaching of the Bible. It has shown us what is important for salvation. Here authoritative guidance was certainly necessary. The Bible does not itself present us with a systemized theology. It is hardly likely to be expected that the average individual would be able by mere reading of the sacred text to arrive at a carefully articulated doctrine of the Incarnation or of the Atonement. We can indeed see St. Paul and the other New Testament writers beginning already to explain the meaning of the events recorded both in the Old and in the New Testaments. The gradual building up of Christian doctrine had thus already begun even within the pages of the Scriptures. The Church has carried on that process and attempted to explain, in the terms of later thought, that which has already been set out in the Scriptures.

Happily the most important part of this work was already done while the Church presented an impressive unity to the world. When doubts were being expressed and saving truth was endangered the Church sent its representatives to meet together and state as concisely as possible what the Bible really did teach. Thus the four great General Councils of Nicea, Constantinople, Ephesus and Chalcedon drew out the doctrine of the nature of God and of the Person of Christ. The views held by the Church in the fourth and fifth centuries were expressed in the terms of Greek philosophy, the best medium of thought available at the time. Its purpose was, of course, not to make belief more difficult, but to make error impossible. Its aim was to avoid mistakes and to give a succinct statement of Christian belief so that people should not be led astray from the path of salvation. It was especially important that they should have a short summary of Christian belief which could easily be memorized. Hence the creeds.

In addition to all this it must be remembered that the Church is not only the means by which God still makes Himself known, but by which God also conveys His own strength and vitality to the lives of men. It is not suggested

that there are no other means by which God can and does
bestow His saving grace, but that this is the covenanted
way. Christ Himself signed the new agreement in His
own Blood, and the Church, as His Body, is still, in spite
of all its failings, the expression of His Person. As His
fleshly body could show weakness and hunger; so the
Church may at times be frail. But, as in the days of His
flesh, Christ found His physical body sufficient to carry
on the authoritative work of His Father, so through the
subsequent ages He has carried on His work of redemption through the Church. 'As my Father hath sent me,
even so send I you.'

6

The third thread of the threefold cord is the individual
conscience. It may be asked what part this can play in
any system of authority. Yet we have only to remember
Kant's famous phrase, 'the categorical imperative,' to
recognize that there is a voice of authority which may
speak in the heart of the individual. That authority must,
in the last resort, be the authority of God Himself. There
are, as we have already suggested, times when God
appears to speak immediately to some great religious
genius. Moses said, 'Would God that all the Lord's
people were prophets.' The early Christians believed that
the pious wish had been fulfilled. The time had come
when they were the privileged recipients of the eternal
Word, who had promised to pour out His Spirit upon all
flesh. They were the people upon whom the ends of the
world had come. We still live under that dispensation of
the Spirit, and consequently everyone of us may believe
that he, too, is privileged to receive indications from God
Himself of His divine Will. There is a voice for us, too,
saying, 'This is the way, walk ye in it.'

Yet it would be a mistake to think that any individual ever does or can act merely upon his own authority. God speaks to us through the universe of our experience. It is well, therefore, if we place ourselves in such an environment and seek such experiences as will help us to distinguish the Voice of God. Conscience is certainly subject to such influences; indeed it ought to be. Left alone and uneducated it would be a very unsafe guide. It can never of itself be an absolutely safe guide. It is no less fallible than any of the other means by which we receive guidance. It requires knowledge of the Bible and training from the Church. It will then give us practical assurance, but only in so far as it has itself been properly conditioned to become an accurate sounding board for the Voice of God.

We repeat, then, that the authority we need is a moral authority and that we can find it in the voice of God speaking through the united witness of Bible, Church, and conscience.

CHAPTER IV

AUTHORITY AND THE INDIVIDUAL

I

THE interest taken by the Church in its individual members is manifested in the simplest and clearest manner by the very first question in the Catechism, 'What is your name?' It is the question that one almost inevitably asks any child with whom one is opening a conversation. Natural as it is, there is embodied in it a profound significance as it is used by the Church. It draws the attention of the child to his own individuality. The name by which he is known distinguishes him from everyone else. The child is assured of his own identity. He is recognized as, in some senses at any rate, the centre of his own universe.

But the name which is expected in the reply is the Christian or given name, not the family name. This shifts the interest from the individual to his spiritual environment. The change is emphasized by the second question, 'Who gave you this name?' Obviously someone has cared enough for the child to give him a distinctive name, and the reply comes that the name was given by the godparents, not the natural parents, but the spiritual parents. It puts the child in relation not merely to society, but to religious society.

This interplay between the child and his surroundings is of fundamental importance. Each reacts upon the other. Psychologists are fond of saying that in the early stages of its development the infant has consciousness of nothing more than being surrounded by a vague blur or an equally vague buzz. The knowledge of its own identity grows as it is able to distinguish itself from this surrounding vagueness. Then by degrees the vagueness takes on distinctive forms of mother or father, cradle or cot, and so on. Without the environment there would probably be no consciousness of self, and without the self there could be no consciousness of an environment. The two play upon each other and are complementary to each other. As the child develops, he begins to realize that there are mutual responsibilities. As he looks to his parents for the supply of his needs, so he becomes conscious that the parents make certain demands upon him. All this becomes obvious and is quite fundamental to natural growth.

The particular interest of the above questions and answers from the Christian point of view is that they make clear to the child that he is the member not of one family only, but of two. In addition to the natural parents, there is the Church in the background, repre-sented by the godparents who gave him his name. The nature of the spiritual family becomes clearer as the child grows old enough to appreciate the meaning of baptism, and realizes the use of the font placed near the entrance of his parish church. These are not fancies, but facts. Godparents are as real as parents. The church building is as substantial as the house in which the child normally lives. The font is as solid as his bath. The representatives of the spiritual life may not be so familiar, but they nevertheless belong to the world of reality and not to the world of make-believe.

There is thus a comparatively easy transition for the child from the recognition of its own home, and the society housed within it, to the idea of a spiritual home

housing a spiritual society. That there is a difference
between the two is obvious. The working out of the distinction forms a large part of the normal child's education.
But the individual is the same in both environments, and
his relationships in both are similar. There is a Heavenly
Father as well as an earthly father, a spiritual as well as
a natural family. The child can look to both for care
and protection and, at the same time, he will be under
obedience to both.

2

Where this train of thought is followed, as it is normally
by those who are brought up in Christian surroundings,
inevitable reflection shows clearly that there is a double
nature in man. The individual is compelled to examine
his own being and to recognize that there is something in
himself corresponding to his double environment. He
would in any case be compelled to recognize that he has
something more than a physical being, that he is not just
made up of flesh and blood. He can very easily recognize
pains and pleasures associated with the body, but he is
conscious also of a whole range of pain and pleasure
revealing no very obvious connection with his physical
being. He develops intellectual, artistic, and even moral
tastes which he can satisfy or fail to satisfy quite indepen-
dently of physical sensations. There is a world of the mind
as well as of the body, in the former of which he can
observe himself thinking, feeling, and willing. This world
of the mind acts as a kind of introduction to a spiritual
existence which he learns to associate with God and
Heaven.

Every normal child develops a keen interest in the unseen world. For a time no doubt there may be a more or
less deliberate building up of a world of make-believe, and

however difficult it may be in later years to recall the fact, the fictional world may for a time appear as real as the material world. The universe, which is sprinkled with fairies and in which dolls appear to have a genuine life, is a kind of stepping-stone to the recognition of an unseen world which exists as truly as the world that is seen and touched and handled. Presently the normal child becomes capable of recognizing the distinction between the true and false, even in this unseen world. 'Is it really true?' is a question which he soon begins to ask, and asks the more insistently as he finds that some of it at any rate is not 'true.' His experience of the beginning and end of life strengthens his interest in this unseen world. 'Where do babies come from?' and 'Where does the pet rabbit go when it dies?' Every parent has had to wrestle with such questions. The reasoning that gives rise to them helps to substantiate the belief in a spiritual existence.

In view of all this it becomes quite natural for the individual to recognize himself as a denizen of two worlds. He belongs to the world of spirit as well as to the world of matter. Thought and teaching enable him to distinguish their characteristics. He recognizes that one is subject to time, the other to eternity. St. Paul says that we are colonists from Heaven, temporary residents in a sphere which is not our true home, looking forward to our return to the country from which we came. Belief in the spiritual is therefore natural to us. It is only by doing violence to his own instincts thus developed that a man can blind himself to the reality of the unseen. Although the claims of the material world are always with him, he has an innate recognition of the fact that the claims of the spiritual are the more important. His immediate necessities may arise in the material sphere, food and clothing and the money needed to procure both. But the real purpose of his existence is not to be found in them. To quote another Catechism, he learns that 'the chief end of man is to glorify God and enjoy Him for ever.'

3

Recognition of this fundamental fact will enable us to avoid the major error of our times. All forms of totalitarianism, whether Fascist or Communist, claim the whole interest of the individual for the State. Indeed, he is not expected to have any aim of his own but to devote himself to the service of the whole. For Christians, of course, there is a familiar sound in this form of words. We, too, are expected to give ourselves to the service of others. But we lose our lives in order to save them. We are promised an enlargement of life and an enhancement of personality. The difference lies in the fact that the totalitarian ends are temporal while the Christian ends are eternal, and therefore infinite. With infinity to draw upon the individual can give his all and yet be enriched.

Christianity does not deny the importance of the State, but regards it as a mere part of the human environment. It does not exist to absorb the individual, but to serve his ends. Man is not like the bee in the hive or the ant on the ant-hill. The whole purpose of his existence is not fulfilled when the material ends of the community have been served. If the individual is a spiritual being, if he has a soul as well as a body, then all temporal and earthly organizations must be intended to serve the higher element of his being, and to assist him in qualifying for his eternal existence. The only claim which can properly demand his complete allegiance on every side of his being is that of eternal Godhead, which is itself mediated by the incarnate Word through His divine Society, the Church.

It is thus in relation to that part of his environment which is constituted by the Church that man reaches his true dignity. It is here that his spiritual needs are satisfied and the true end of his being receives proper emphasis. The Church, as the Body of Christ, is 'the universal means of expression of a Universal Personality.'[1] When a child is baptized he is, as St. Paul says, 'grafted into' that Personality. The life, the vital energy of Christ, flows through his veins just as the sap of a tree flows through the twig which has been grafted into it. Everything in the Church serves to emphasize this living relationship with Christ. At Confirmation the baptized Christian receives a new access of the Spirit of Christ. In the Holy Communion he is strengthened with the Body and Blood, the personal character and the vital energy of Christ. At each succeeding stage of his life, it is the Church that blesses him, and so presents itself as the instrument by which strength is given him for the full performance of the duties required of him.

The true environment of the Christian is therefore Christ Himself. It is in Him alone that the individual can develop to that perfection to which he has been called and so attain the true end of his being. We can understand more easily what this involves if we grasp firmly the meaning of the Resurrection. In the risen Christ we see human nature raised to its proper glory. If the individual is united to Christ he shares with Him both His death to sin and His new life to righteousness. As the acorn, given the proper atmosphere and the proper nourishment, develops into the oak, so the Christian having been made partaker of the divine nature

[1] Eph. i. 22 (Wand, *New Testament Letters*, p. 114).

can attain to the full meaning of human nature as it is revealed in the risen Christ. 'God became man,' St. Athanasius dared to say, 'in order that we might become God.'

4

From all this we can learn the true nature of the obedience expected from the individual. It is not mere observance of a rule, but attachment to a Person. So long as we acknowledge allegiance to Christ we have the opportunity of continual advance. So long as we are in Christ our progress is a continual growth. 'The path of the righteous is as the light of dawn which shineth more and more unto the perfect day.' This does not mean that there can never be any clouds over the sun. We are capable of mistakes and we have no guarantee that we shall always do right, but the light still shines and the ultimate future is assured. We are at least saved from the agonized striving after virtues that appear to be foreign to us. We are not forever struggling after some goal that is beyond our reach. The life of Christ within us must grow towards maturity so long as we recognize our oneness with Him.

At the same time we are subject to loving correction. In this respect, too, Christ uses His Church as the instrument of His personal action. The duty of discipline has been laid upon the Church by Christ Himself. There must be some meaning in His words, which are still repeated at the Ordination of a priest, 'Whosesoever sins thou dost remit they are remitted unto him, and whosesoever sins thou dost retain, they are retained.' The least they can mean is that we must accept as authoritative within the terms of time and space the Church's judgement on our moral lives.

This, of course, involves the possibility of penalties for wrong-doing. There is even in the last resort the dread possibility of excommunication. If we prove completely self-willed and recalcitrant, the divine society, like any other society, can 'send us to Coventry' and refuse to admit us to its privileges until we come to a better mind. To this we must be ready to submit. It is, after all, only a proper recognition of the obligations resting upon the divine family. If we are adopted into the family, we must be willing to behave as members of it. The Father has the right to ask so much of His children. And we can do it. God has given us all the strength we need. He never calls upon us to do anything of which with His aid we are not capable. The life of Christ within us is the guarantee of continued power. We can never fail altogether unless we deliberately sever ourselves from Him.

The obedience that we owe to the divine society is, of course, not absolute in the sense that we are expected to do everything that can ever be demanded of us whatever the nature of the command. It is no more absolute than is the obedience of the bride to the husband whom she promises to obey. She can be expected to obey only so long as the husband's demands are in accordance with the true character of marriage. If the Church, or any officer of it, were to ask us to do something that was not in accordance with the law of God, we should not be expected to obey. All we are asked to do is to 'observe the rules of the game.' Such obedience is what is known theologically as 'canonical' obedience. It is obedience according to the rules or canons, obedience within the proper nature and constitution of the Christian society.

5

There falls for consideration another aspect of the truth that only in obedience to the claims of God can the individual fully develop his own personality. It is that God demands of us not merely some particular part of our life which we can regard as specifically 'religious,' but the whole. It is not only the moments we spend in prayer or the hour that we devote to worship which must be given to God, but our everyday employment whether in work or leisure.

The fact is that God has a place for each of us in His plan for the universe. There is a niche for each one of us to fill, and we miss our vocation if we fail to fill it. The logical result follows that it is our business to find out precisely what it is God wants us to do. We are commonly accustomed to recognize that the minister, the monk, and the missionary have each a special vocation from God. The same is equally true of the butcher, the baker, and the candlestick maker. No man has any right to decide the course of his life merely in accordance with some desire he may have for the easiest possible time, nor has he any right to make a decision merely in accordance with the need for earning a livelihood. No doubt our private tastes, our innate skills, and our comparative poverty, may help us to decide in what direction God is calling us. We may be assisted to know His will by the advice of parents, teachers, and friends. But with or without such aid we ought in the last resort to know beyond possibility of mistake what God Himself is calling us to do.

Only so can we guarantee any genuine happiness in our choice of a career. Indeed, if our career is a vocation, that is a 'call,' we cannot choose it. You do not choose a call, you merely answer it. The matter is very serious for the individual. If there is scarcely any happiness to be compared with the knowledge that we are engaged upon the one task God has given us to perform, there is scarcely any misery to be compared with that of knowing that we have, as we say, 'mistaken our vocation.'

It is well if in addition to thus accepting direction from God as to our profession, we can consecrate the work of our lives by devoting some special time to specific Church work. The principle of using a part in order to hallow the whole is well-rooted in the Biblical way of life. The setting apart of one day in each week for the special worship of God was intended to cast a halo about every day. Ezekiel's plan for the restored Israel was built upon the idea that the allocation of one piece of land for the sanctuary of God would hallow the whole national territory. In the same way the setting apart of the tribe of the Levites as God's ministers was intended to emphasize the fact that the whole nation was engaged in the service of God. So if we can give some part of our time, however small, to doing some definite piece of work for the Church, we shall confirm the fact that our whole work, however secular it may seem, is still something done in pursuance of a call from God.

Certainly we shall be helped by such means to realize that the Church does not consist of the clergy alone and that Church work is not their exclusive prerogative. God's *laos* or people includes both clergy and laity; and each section has a necessary part to play in the functioning of the whole. Particularly is it necessary to remember this in days when the disproportion between the number of the clergy and that of the laity is increasing. During the last thirty years the nation has added fifteen millions to its population, while the total number of clergy has decreased by five thousand. It is obvious that if the work

D

of the Church is to be done on anything like the old scale, it can only be as the laity shoulder a good many of the responsibilities that have hitherto been borne by the clergy.

Happily there are signs that the laity are recognizing this claim of God upon them and are submitting to it with ever greater willingness. It would be safe to say that a number of the recent evangelistic efforts made in various large centres of population would have been impossible if it had not been for the fact that the laity undertook a good deal of the preliminary work of house-to-house visiting. Further, there is a growing recognition in parochial church councils and in such bodies as the Church of England Men's Society that there is very much in the ordinary day-to-day work of the Church which can be undertaken by the laity. Consequently there is probably at the moment a closer co-operation between clergy and laity in the one common task than there has ever been before in the history of the Church.

It can be seen that the picture of the Christian life presented to us in the Church is very far from an atomic individualism. The individual is important: indeed, of paramount importance, because it is individual souls that God creates and our Lord came to redeem. But the individual soul cannot attain to perfection in isolation. Our true happiness depends very largely upon our relation to society. In living a social life we have no doubt to put up with many difficulties and disappointments. There is continual onslaught upon our affections, our patience, and our faith in humanity. Nevertheless all this is necessary for the perfection of our own development. If we cut ourselves off from our fellows, our personality becomes withered, shrunken and near to atrophy. Society has a definite claim upon us, and we cannot achieve our end without recognizing that claim. In particular we must, if we wish to be in the way of salvation, recognize the claim of the divine society. We are, as St. Peter says, living stones in a spiritual temple.[1] It is only as we accept our proffered place in that construction that we can attain satisfaction. It is only so that the whole building can continue to progress, and that God can be adequately served.

[1] 1 Pet. ii. 5.

CHAPTER V

INTELLECTUAL AUTHORITY

I

ONE of the questions addressed to every candidate for admission into the Christian Church concerns his belief. The Church of England, like all other denominations, claims an authority in settling what must be believed by its members. As the vehicle of an authoritative revelation from God it can, of course, do no less. Even a secular society must see that its members accept the terms of association. Because religion is concerned so largely with the inner man it must make a special point of belief. There has been in England far too long a popular idea that it does not matter what a man believes and that a church ought to be able to dispense with dogmatic statements. It is necessary, however, to point out that belief is of the utmost importance, because, so long as we are sincere, what we believe will inevitably dictate our conduct. Also it must be remembered that no society of any kind can exist except on the basis of some common belief. Even a society of atheists would presumably have the one common platform that there is no God, and anyone who could not accept that platform would be disqualified for admission into the society.

The popular prejudice, however, is not so much against belief itself as against its dogmatic formulation. That is very largely due to failure to recognize that every belief clearly held must be formulated. Religious ideas must be brought out of the region of vague sentiment into that of definite statement. We need therefore entertain no prejudice against dogma. It is true that we dislike a dogmatic *person*, but that is merely because he gives to his own private judgement the force of an official and authorized statement. Such a person is quite properly intolerable because he usurps for himself a place that belongs to the community. But official and authorized statements must of necessity be dogmatic. They come with the whole authority of the society behind them, and it is to everybody's interest that they should be as clear and precise as possible. Any Christian society that dispenses with creeds loses its power to define its beliefs and comes very near to the final surrender of Christianity both as a historical religion and as an identifiable attitude to life.

If it is complained that the creeds, as we have them, are too theological, the answer is that theology is only thinking about religion. If we really wish to think any subject out thoroughly, we must analyse and examine it, and get our thoughts about it so clear that we can express our conclusions tersely and concisely. Any failure so to state them would mean that we had not thought the subject through. The creeds are such concise conclusions, showing the results of revelation and of careful thinking about it. They are a compendium of theology.

We need have no fear that in demanding acceptance of her officially authorized statements the Church is endeavouring to destroy our own right of judgement. Ultimately what she wishes to do is to commend herself to everyone's conscience in the sight of God. The conscience of the individual must in the long run decide for itself. Even if in the beginning it is the godparents who have decided on behalf of a baby, yet the baby is given the chance of individual decision as soon as it arrives at the age of discretion; and at any moment in later life it can still exercise its right of personal choice. In that sense there is no conflict between the intellectual authority of the Church and private judgement. When a conflict arises it is much more likely to be because the private judgement is exercised in an ignorant fashion without giving due weight to the age-long experience of the Church. No doubt the rare occasion will arise when a man must defy public opinion and say, 'Here stand I, I can do no other.' Then patience will be needed to see whether his teaching is of God. In any case ideas can only be met by ideas, and he should submit his views to public examination. Private judgement is only illegitimate when it denies the claim of society to express the common mind of its members.

A more reasonable ground of misunderstanding is sometimes to be found in the ambiguity of the word 'belief.' Intellectual assent is normally applied to the acceptance of a fact, or of a statement. There is, however, another kind of belief which means moral trust in a person or institution. You may say that you believe the Battle of Waterloo was fought in 1815, or you may say that you believe in President Truman. Obviously the two types of belief are very different. It is to be noticed that, as far as the creeds are concerned, although the acceptance of certain historical facts is expected, it is the second kind of belief that is mostly envisaged. One says, 'I believe *in* God.' Therefore what we are concerned with in the creeds is an outgoing of the whole personality rather than a mere cold assent of the discursive reason. It is faith rather than knowledge which is demanded.

This distinction is already drawn clearly in the New Testament. Belief, in the sense of intellectual assent, is not enough. 'The devils also believe and tremble.' At the same time it must be noticed that even from the point of view of the creed a certain measure of intellectual assent is necessary. You cannot believe in God without first believing that God exists. Even if in the creeds you begin by saying, 'I believe in God,' or 'in Jesus Christ,' you soon go on to describe them as doing certain things which you accept as historical facts.

Naturally no one would wish to make intellectual assent harder than is necessary, or to make it cover a wider range of facts than are required as a basis for the scheme of salvation. That is why the Church has in point of fact kept her creeds to a minimum. When you think of the vast range of interests they are expected to cover, when you remember the manifold variety of possible activities, human and divine, and when you think how many are the pitfalls into which one may be led by ignorance, wilfulness or perverted judgement, it will seem little short of amazing that these short, simple statements should be considered sufficient. The fact is, of course, that these creeds are not intended to cover every doubtful point. They are meant as signposts indicating the right way for the believer to walk. They follow the method of 'safety first.' They are deliberately intended to keep the pilgrim on the safe road, and to prevent him from turning into dangerous by-paths. So far from being worked up in order to make things difficult for the over-conscientious or to titillate the imagination of the merely curious, they have the plain practical intention of giving the Christian confidence that he possesses the basic information necessary for the saving way of life and for the pleasure of proclaiming it to all who care to hear.

2

It is not to be supposed that the creeds emerged in completely articulated form at the beginning of Christian history. It is certain that they developed from small and primitive beginnings. Probably the earliest statement of faith was simply a declaration that Jesus is Lord. St. Paul, in fact, tells us that no one can make that statement wholeheartedly unless he is inspired to do so by the Holy Spirit.[1] It looks, therefore, as if it were a form of words recognized as crucially important to which Christians were accustomed almost from the first to give expression. We know, too, that a baptism was customarily performed in the Name of Jesus. As baptism was the ceremony by which the neophyte was initiated into the Church, he could properly be expected to make some statement of his faith on such an occasion. A declaration that Jesus is Lord would enable the ceremony to be described as baptism in or into the Name of Jesus. And that, we know, was the customary description in New Testament times. In any case that there was a very close connection between the declaration of belief in Jesus, and the ceremony of Christian baptism is made very clear in Acts viii. 37, where, according to one familiar reading, the Ethiopian eunuch was told that he could be baptized if he had the right belief, and he replied, 'I believe that Jesus Christ is the Son of God.'

This connection with initiation soon involved an enrichment of the creed. Baptism was not always just into the Name of Jesus. We know from the concluding words of St. Matthew's Gospel that it was a very early custom to baptize in the threefold Name of the Father, the Son, and the Holy Spirit. There is every reason to believe

[1] 1 Cor. xii. 3.

that just as the eunuch was asked about his belief before being baptized into the Name of Jesus, so others would be asked about their belief before being baptized into the threefold Name of Father, Son, and Holy Spirit. The conclusion is almost inevitable that they would give their answer in a threefold form. That certainly is the form which was followed by the creeds as they developed in later years. There was a further reason for this development. In addition to the questions asked at the actual baptism, there was a preliminary period of training for the catechumens. They were taught to state their Christian belief in a few simple words which they learnt by heart. Naturally this statement also followed the three-fold form. It was out of a combination of the pre-baptismal training with the reply to the question asked at baptism that the Creed we now know as the Apostles' Creed developed. It was, of course, not composed by the Apostles, although a legend soon grew to that effect. Nevertheless we can be assured that it does incorporate and summarize the Apostles' teaching; and that is perhaps sufficient to justify the name.

The teaching of the catechumens was in the hands of the bishops. Each bishop would follow his own syllabus of teaching. From time to time he would expand the Creed in order to include some special point upon which he had found it necessary to insist. Consequently there grew up various forms of the Creed, each of which was associated either with a particular bishop or a particular see. This varied expansion had considerable importance when the Church entered into the period during which her faith was subject to intense examination under the influence of Greek philosophical thought. When it was felt that some bishops had strayed from the straight path of doctrinal accuracy, councils were gathered to decide what was the official teaching of the whole Church. Bishops were then expected to give some proof of their orthodoxy; and the easiest way to do it was to produce the creed they were accustomed to deliver to their own catechumens. That would be the best available evidence of their characteristic teaching. From this it was very easy to take the step of authorizing an official creed to serve as a test of orthodoxy for all bishops. The most important occasion on which this was done was the first Œcumenical Council held at Nicea in 325. Indeed, on that occasion the bishops not only stated positively in the body of the creed what was the accepted doctrine, but they added an appendix of various anathemas against different types of false teaching. In this way the bishops who signed this creed gave a twofold assurance of their orthodoxy, positive and negative. They stated both what they did teach and what they did not. Subsequently the anathemas dropped out. When the new enlarged creed was taken over into public worship at the Eucharist, it only stated the accepted belief in a positive form. But it still followed the threefold scheme, expanding in an explanatory way the views held by Christians about the Father, Son, and Holy Spirit.

This is a sufficient account for the present of the Apostles' and the 'Nicene' creeds. What we know as the Athanasian Creed is not really a creed at all, and it was certainly not composed by Athanasius. Something of the spirit of the old anathemas has crept into it, and this is the strongest reason for its present lack of popularity. The liturgiologist has a stronger reason for declining to call it a creed. It departs from the threefold scheme and contents itself with a twofold form. The first part deals with the doctrine of the Trinity, the second part deals with the doctrine of Christ. Both are admirably done so far as they go, but they are incomplete even apart from the omission of the Holy Spirit. The second part, while it refutes heretical notions about Christ, shows no knowledge of heresy on this particular head beyond the comparatively early years of controversy. It stops short before Apollinarianism became a vogue with its teaching of a defective manhood in Christ. Many scholars suppose that it may have been written as a kind of Hymn of Faith by St. Ambrose of Milan before the close of the fourth century. It does not possess the conciliar authority of the 'Nicene' Creed.

3

It will be realized from this brief description that each of the three creeds has a special character of its own.

The Apostles' Creed consists mostly of factual statements. The second part of it consists of an outline of the life of Christ, and even the third section, although it adds the Church, the forgiveness of sins, and the resurrection to the statement about the Holy Spirit, mentions them merely as bare facts without defining their doctrinal significance. This, of course, is much the simplest of the creeds at present in use. For that reason, as well as for its severely factual character, it is the most widely accepted throughout Christendom to-day. There are even some denominations which accept it alone of all the creeds and refuse to make any further demands upon their members.

The Church of England, on the other hand, in common with the historic churches of Christendom, accepts also the Nicene Creed, employing it as an instrument of worship rather than as a test for entrance into the Church. The reason why objection is sometimes taken to it is that it is not content with merely stating the facts, but tries to give some philosophical explanation of them. The central clause is that which describes Jesus Christ as of 'one substance with the Father,' meaning that Christ shares in the essential nature of Godhead. It is contended that this changes the character of the demand made upon the individual. Instead of being asked to accept the basic historic facts upon which Christianity is built, he is required to affirm a doctrinal formula.

To that objection, however, the answer may be given that facts do not exist in a vacuum. They are related to all kinds of causes and consequences. As is often said, there is no fact without value. What the Nicene Creed is doing is to state what the Church believes to have been revealed about the values of certain facts. It is to be noted that the Church did not take this action unprovoked and of its own volition. Certain teachers had stated the wrong kind of values and it could not escape the necessity of proclaiming the right ones. We may be grateful that we should have been privileged to receive so clear a statement of the mind of the undivided Church which, whatever differences it caused at the time, was reiterated by succeeding œcumenical councils, and confirmed by the common consent of Christian opinion.

In the Athanasian Creed this process is carried farther, but along the lines of Latin rather than Greek theology. It provides a typical example of Latin rhetoric, proceeding by the way of statement and antithesis, and showing very little of the subtlety characteristic of Greek thought. It is, of course, very easy to poke fun at its repetitive statements about the three and the one, but that superficial type of criticism went out with the eighteenth century. Modern thinkers are prepared to see a much closer approximation to reality in the Church's method of stating her belief than in the easy agnosticism of Victorian liberals. A more

valid objection can be brought against what are generally
called the damnatory clauses. But the word 'damnatory'
is tendentious and not strictly justified. The precise
meaning comes out much more clearly in the Latin
original than in the English translation. It is, perhaps,
impossible, even if desirable, to get rid altogether of the
harshness with which the penalties of unbelief are
expressed, but at least it should be noted that the hymn is
not calling down curses but stating logical consequences.
It is valuable to have a warning that belief is of fundamental importance, and that if we wish to continue in the
path of safety without jeopardizing our eternal salvation
it is necessary to think of God and His nature in certain
ways. That is really what the Athanasian Creed sets out
to give, and there is a growing appreciation of its value
in this respect.

4

It is interesting to notice that these creeds belong to the
fourth and fifth centuries of Christian history. That was
a great age of creed-making, when the faith was being
subtly challenged and had to be defended. We have to
travel eleven hundred years before we come to a period of
equal challenge and of equal activity in meeting the
challenge. The period of the Reformation involved the
splitting up of the mediæval unity into many national
churches, with a consequential effort on the part of each
to assert its own belief in its own terms. It is interesting
that practically all of them acted on the assumption
that the earlier creeds must be accepted as foundation
documents whose teaching was not in dispute. They did
not try to replace them, but put beside them elaborate
confessions of faith mostly concerned with new points of
controversy. Great differences of opinion had arisen

about the nature of man and about the scheme of salvation, about Church authority, and about the sacraments. The Westminster Confession, the Confession of Augsburg, and the Decrees of the Council of Trent, may be mentioned as three examples of the way in which different sections of Christendom stated the belief to which they expected their own members to give unqualified consent.

The Church of England did not escape this tendency, but declared its own faith in the Thirty-nine Articles. We must say a word about their content and about the demand they make upon us. Those who like to ridicule what they believe to be the illogical position of Anglicanism sometimes say that, while we have a Catholic Prayer Book, we have an Erastian ministry and Calvinistic articles. There is just enough truth in this aphorism to make it amusing. But it certainly is not strictly true that the Thirty-nine Articles are Calvinist. Indeed, some of the most specific 'Reformed' doctrines are implicitly repudiated. The articles on predestination, on the depravity of human nature, and on the lack of freedom in the human will are all grave understatements from the Calvinist point of view. It is, indeed, generally agreed that Newman was right in his famous Tract 90 when he contended that the Thirty-nine Articles were capable of a Catholic interpretation. Nevertheless it would be useless to deny the generally 'Reformed' tone of the Articles. Dom Gregory Dix in his valuable little book, *The Question of Anglican Orders*, has recognized the difficulty of saying precisely where Catholicism ends and Protestantism begins. He finds the line of demarcation in the doctrine of justification by faith alone. We may, perhaps, think that he has over-simplified the issue, but nevertheless it is important to notice that if that must be taken as the dividing line, then the Thirty-nine Articles are *formally* on the Protestant side of it.

It is doubtful, however, whether Anglican theologians ever meant by 'justification' all that continental theologians included in that term. A close investigation of the meaning of justification and its relation to sanctification and salvation would probably show that even Article XI is more Catholic than Calvinist. We might contrast that much more typically Protestant statement, the Westminster Confession, which emphasizes predestination rather than baptism. However, this is a technical matter into which we have no space to enter now.

In addition to the creeds and articles there is a further help that the Anglican receives in the explication of his faith and its application to current questions. This is to be found in the encyclical letters, the reports and resolutions of the Lambeth Conference. This Conference is not, strictly speaking, authoritative. It is a gathering of Anglican bishops from all over the world who meet every ten years or so to discuss contemporary problems. Whatever recommendations are made by them only become authoritative when they are accepted by national, provincial, or diocesan councils. Obviously, however, whatever is agreed upon by the bishops of a whole Communion must have great weight as what the lawyers call 'persuasive precedents.' At the lowest estimate they give advice which is extremely valuable, not only to clergy but also to laity who wish to avail themselves of the accumulated experiences of so many chief pastors in so many different lands. The reports generally begin with the examination of some particular theological question and go on to point out its application to the practical issues agitating people's minds at the moment. Later examination by experienced theologians often reveals some flaw in the argument, but the cumulative effect of the findings is considerable, and they bring relief to many who are perplexed and are looking for guidance in private or public difficulties.

5

It will be gathered that the intellectual authority exercised by the Church varies in weight and character. Not all its utterances involve the same degree of obligation. It is not merely that there is a clear-cut distinction between matters of faith and pious opinions. There are many different levels of authority. The Apostles' Creed is universally received in the West. The Nicene Creed has behind it the binding force of the whole undivided Church. The Athanasian Creed has not the same conciliar authority and there is room for considerable difference of opinion about the precise meaning and weight of the so-called damnatory clauses, but the doctrinal exposition is accepted as authoritative so far as it goes. The Thirty-nine Articles, on the other hand, are peculiar to the Church of England. They are not intended to have the same binding force on the conscience. The clergy, when they are ordained or take a fresh post, have to assent to them. That declaration of assent does not mean that the clergy must accept them as a sufficient statement of Christian doctrine. It means that they agree to accept them as a basis of teaching and not to teach anything contrary to them. It is questionable how far they are binding on the laity at all. No doubt the laity are expected to recognize them as the norm of Anglican doctrine and they listen to them as they are read by incumbents when they take up duty in a new benefice. Apart from that the laity can scarcely be said to have any responsibility in connection with them. Finally, the

Lambeth resolutions have no binding force at all, unless, and until, they are officially accepted by the duly constituted ecclesiastical authority of a diocese, province, or country.

It would be a pity, however, if we left the impression that statements of belief were meant to exercise constraint on unwilling minds. It is, of course, true that they are intended to mark the limits within which credence is expected from members of the Church. But faith is not unwilling. It is a glad acceptance of revealed truth. It comes as the result of complete trust in the Person of Christ and the good order He has taken for His people. A creed is the jubilant expression of this faith. It is the symbol or watchword of the Christian soldier. It is repeated with joy and gratitude. It should be chanted in the same triumphant tone as that in which Frenchmen once sang the 'Marseillaise.' It is our marching song. We know that as we accept it and live in its spirit we shall be led to ultimate victory in the battle of individual life and in the age-long war of good against evil.

E

CHAPTER VI

THE AUTHORITY OF THE SACRAMENTS

I

IT might be thought at first sight that a discussion of the sacraments in this context would be a digression. This is not so. The sacraments are just as much a part of the authoritative system of the Church as the creeds. The task of the Church is to continue the Lord's twofold work of revelation and redemption. If the creeds are a concise summary of the facts of revelation, the sacraments are an epitome of Christ's work of redemption. That work is carried out by the application of the life of Christ to the believer. The sacraments are the authorized means of that application.

It is sometimes suggested that the sacraments are in some way opposed to a truly spiritual religion. They have to do with material means whereas religion should be purely a concern of the spirit. This is a false and unnecessary opposition. It is certainly true, as we have insisted over and over again, that God can and does speak directly to the human soul, but it is equally true that normally He uses media of one kind or another. Commonly, of course, He uses the human personality. He speaks to us through the agency of parents, ministers, teachers or friends; and, in so far as He does this, the human agents are themselves a kind of sacrament. The influence of personality is generally exerted through physical and material means such as the body and the words, gestures or acts of the body. There is no necessary opposition therefore between what is sometimes called a prophetic and a priestly religion, a religion which relies upon words and a religion which relies upon acts.

What we know as the sacraments *par excellence* are authoritative because they are covenanted means of grace. As such they have a claim upon the individual. He must accept them and use them if he is a faithful servant of Christ. He can no more dispense with them than he can with his prayers or the reading of the Bible. Of two of them at least, generally known as the Gospel Sacraments, it is claimed in the Catechism that 'they were ordained by Christ Himself.' The last verses of St. Matthew's Gospel depict the risen Christ as bidding His followers 'make disciples of all the nations, baptizing them in the name of the Father, the Son, and the Holy Ghost.' With regard to the other, the Holy Communion, there is, of course, no doubt that Jesus participated in the Last Supper with His Disciples, and it is in the repetition of His acts on that occasion that the sacrament of the Eucharist originates. The sacraments are therefore authoritative just as the creeds are authoritative. Indeed, the Gospel sacraments have a more direct authorization from Christ than the creeds.

2

The definition of a sacrament is 'the outward and visible sign of an inward and spiritual grace given unto us.' It represents the conjunction of material means with spiritual power. The term 'sign' is used in the particular sense, not of a mere empty symbol, but of an effective instrument by means of which the grace is given. It is a sign not in the sense in which the Royal Standard flying over Buckingham Palace is a sign that the King is in residence, but in the sense in which certain fittings are a sign that electric light and power are available in the house. The flag does not bring the King, but the wiring is the actual means by which the power is conveyed. As the Catechism says, the sacrament is a sign of grace not only as 'the pledge to assure us thereof,' but also a 'means whereby we receive the same.'

The sacramental approach to religion is not characteristic of the Christian Church only. It is also to be found, though this is sometimes denied, in the Old Testament. There the bestowal of spiritual gifts is associated with objects, gestures and words. Such association was especially easy for the Hebrew people, because they did not, as we do, separate sharply between the material and the spiritual. Indeed, the Old Testament writers describe material things as being themselves vital in a way far transcending anything that would be characteristic of our common thought to-day. They not only thought of each limb of the human frame as possessing a life of its own, but it was normal for them to describe the blood as being life itself. Apart from this particular Hebraism in relation to blood, everyone is aware of the mysterious quality the Hebrew ascribed to the religious use of oil. No doubt its refreshing property when applied to the skin in a hot climate assisted in the development of such an association. Similarly they believed that gestures could be used to convey spiritual gifts. For instance, the laying on of the hand could convey blessing and authority. Again, words were thought of as possessing a special power of their own. A name was not just a label attached to a person, but it included in a mysterious way the personality itself, so that if you knew a person's name you could acquire power over him. Again, a word of command was regarded as carrying the creative force of a person beyond the reach of his physical grasp. 'By the Word of the Lord were the Heavens made, and all the hosts of them by the breath of His mouth.'

This last instance suggests the rationale of this type of thought. A word incorporated the breath of the person who spoke, and that breath was his spirit or personal force. Similarly gestures and objects were regarded as being permeated by a spirit or personality when they were used either by God or under His authority. Thus for the Hebrew there was no impassable gulf between the material and the spiritual: the spiritual pervaded the material. The importance of all this is that the same type of thought still prevails in the New Testament. It was given a new direction by Jesus who associated it not only with the Spirit of God, but with Himself, and so imbued it with a new richness of personal equality: spiritual power takes on the features of Christ. That is the background against which we must understand Baptism and Holy Communion and indeed all the sacraments.

This is the answer to those who assert that the Christian sacraments were borrowed from the mystery cults of paganism. No one disputes that the same type of general thought is to be found in these cults, but there is not the slightest reason to suppose that the New Testament borrowed its ideas from them. In fact, so clear are the New Testament writers that what they say is in line with their own traditions and the teaching of Christ that they do not attempt to disguise the obvious parallels between the Christian sacraments and the rites of paganism. St. Paul can thus compare the Breaking of Bread with both Jewish and pagan sacrifices. He does not say that there is no truth in the pagan sacramentalism. What he does say is that you cannot eat of the table of the Lord and of the table of devils. In either case you are in touch with spiritual powers, but in one case it is with the Spirit of Christ, and in the other it is with the spirit of evil.

The doubt whether matter can be used in order to convey spiritual grace is a modern one which would have had no meaning for the ancients. In the Scriptures, the foundation documents of the Christian Church, the two are associated in the clearest possible manner. What God has joined together let no man put asunder. The only question that remains is as to the way by which the spiritual gift reaches the believer when associated with material means. Does it come, so to speak, through the natural substance, gesture or word, or does it unfailingly reach the believer direct from Heaven on the occasion when the substance, gesture or word is employed? The question is a purely academic one and need not detain us here. All we are concerned to contend is that the spiritual reality is associated with the physical means when rightly employed under the authority of Christ.

Nor has the charge that the sacraments partake of the nature of magic any greater force. There is a whole world of difference between magic and Christian sacraments. The purpose of magic is to bend the unseen forces to our will. The magician, it has been well said, behaves like the conductor of an orchestra compelling the invisible powers to do his bidding. In Christian worship, on the other hand, the whole purpose is to put the believer under the control of God. It is not even the priest who is the real celebrant of the Christian mysteries, but Christ Himself. All is subordinate to Him. It is under His authority that we act, and it is His power that gives us the promised grace. Thus magic is not even a blasphemous parody of sacraments: it is their direct contradiction.

3

Christian tradition after long hesitation about the number of the sacraments, has singled out seven as specially authorized. Some sections of the Church regard them all as being expressly ordered by Christ. The Anglican Church does not go so far, but sets the Gospel Sacraments on a special plane as alone having a 'visible sign or ceremony ordained of God.' Of the rest we may believe that they flow from the will of Christ either as expressed by Him directly or as revealed in the example of the Apostles. It is not to be supposed that men who acted under His authority and whose lives were consecrated to the fulfilment of His will would depart knowingly from His intention. In marriage a custom which had existed long before the beginning of the Christian dispensation was now given a special connotation 'in Christ.' The unction of the sick is prescribed by St. James in terms which suggest that it was a common practice.[1] The reconciliation of the penitent was soon to rest upon our Lord's words, 'Whosesoever sins ye remit they are remitted unto them.'

Confirmation was part of the Christian rite of initiation. The practice of the laying on of hands for the reception of the Holy Spirit was regarded as the natural corollary of baptism and, together with Holy Communion, as the completion of that rite. By the Book of Common Prayer it is ordered in the instruction given to godparents at the baptism of an infant and in the rubric regulating admission to Holy Communion. It can fairly be said that in its method of administering this sacrament the Anglican

[1] The 'corrupt following of the Apostles' referred to in Article XXV probably applies to the relegation of this sacrament to the end of life as 'Extreme Unction.'

Church is nearer to primitive custom than any other church in Christendom.

As for Baptism, because it was 'generally necessary to salvation' it was administered with considerable freedom. It was evidently regarded as proper to throw the gate of entry into the Church as wide open as possible. Consequently all through the Christian centuries the tendency has been to make Baptism easy. To-day there is very considerable criticism of the freedom with which we still minister it in this country. Since it is so commonly given to infants there is an obvious danger that the children, having once been admitted to the Church, may fail to fulfil those promises made on their behalf by their godparents. That danger has not been escaped under modern conditions. In England 66 per cent of the children are brought to the clergy of the national Church for baptism, but a considerable proportion of them do not go on to Confirmation, and an even greater proportion fail to become regular communicants. This is an obvious evil, and the suggestion is made that we should refuse to admit children to baptism unless we have some kind of guarantee that they will be brought up as practising Christians. On the other side it is replied that the remedy might prove worse than the disease. By preventing parents and godparents from bringing children to baptism except on rigorous terms, we might sever the precarious hold that a large proportion of the population still has on Christian life and Church membership. How the difficulty is to be solved we cannot yet see, but at least the teaching of the Church of England is clear that children should be brought to Baptism and that they should be brought to the Bishop to be confirmed by him when they have received the rudiments of Christian teaching and are capable of making a decision of their own.

With regard to the Holy Communion, a somewhat different line has been taken. The Table of the Lord has been fenced about so as to make an unworthy approach difficult, if not impossible. Sacramental communion has been regarded as an inner mystery of the Christian Faith, and therefore only those who are wholehearted in their Christian profession are admitted to it. Curiously enough many people do not seem to be so conscious of the necessity of this sacrament as they are in the case of Baptism. Yet throughout the history of the Church it has been regarded as the Christian service *par excellence*. Baptism and Confirmation occur only once in a lifetime, but the Eucharist frequently. The reason why there is a lack of a sense of obligation in this particular instance may be that during their early years many Christians are unaccustomed to the regular use of sacramental means of grace. Much stress has been laid upon the necessity for prayer and Bible-reading, while as unconfirmed members of the Church they have not been allowed to make their Communion, and many of them are even unfamiliar with the Eucharistic liturgy. Thus they have grown up without adequate recognition of the need for sacraments. If during their early life they have gone for so long without sacraments, why should they later be required to regard participation in them as fundamentally necessary? There is an obvious difficulty here, but it may be answered that in human life increasing responsibility involves the need for increased strength. As we enter adolescence and the world enlarges its claims upon us we need fresh means to enable us to maintain our Christian witness. There is something to be said for not introducing the child to all its privileges at once. God did not reveal Himself all at once to the human race, but by stages as they were able to assimilate His teaching until at last the full revelation was given in His Son. So in the case of the individual, new means of grace are put at his disposal when he has learned something of the difficulties of practical life and has come to realize how much support he needs.

4

One of the objections sometimes brought against the sacramental system is that it is not ethical. Valid sacraments, it is said, do not depend upon the moral character either of the minister or of the recipient. So long as the technical requirements are fulfilled, grace is made available and bestowed. This, so far as it goes, is true. But a moment's reflection will show that to make the value of the sacraments depend upon the moral character of the minister would be in effect largely to destroy it. It would mean that the faithful could never be sure whether they were receiving the covenanted help from God, because they would never be certain that the minister was a good enough person to be an effective agent. It belongs inevitably to the character of a sacrament that the worshipper should be sure that he receives the promised help. That he can be, if he knows that the required conditions have been fulfilled. This implies that once you accept the view that spiritual help can be given by material means, then you must allow the material means to follow the law of their own nature. Both in form and matter they must obey prescribed rules. When that is done you are assured that you receive the covenanted grace. Unless that is true a sacrament is no sacrament at all.

But it may be objected that it is still unethical to suggest that a person can receive divine grace without any regard to his own moral character. Apart altogether from the character of the minister, it is suggested, surely the recipient must satisfy moral requirements. There is a sense in which this is undoubtedly true, but here a distinction must be clearly drawn between reception and effective reception. If we receive the outward and visible sign, we receive also the inward and spiritual grace, but unless we are in the right moral attitude this reception will not be an effective reception. It will, that is to say, do us no good and may even do us harm, because we shall have added sacrilege to our other faults. St. Paul makes it quite clear that in his view unworthy reception of the Holy Communion brings punishment in its train. 'For this cause many are sickly among you and some sleep.' In other words the sacramental gift may be received, but it may not be effective, because of the impediment set up by the unbelief or impenitence of the recipient.

It is for this reason that such strong emphasis is placed upon the necessity for a right disposition on the part of those who receive the sacraments. For Baptism, repentance and faith are required. Of those who come to Holy Communion it is required that they should examine themselves, 'whether they repent them truly of their former sins, steadfastly purposing to lead a new life; have a lively faith in God's mercy through Christ, with a thankful remembrance of His Death; and be in charity with all men.' Similarly in regard to all the sacraments, if we are to benefit from them it is necessary that we should have a definite belief in their value and a real determination to use the promised help.

When the Sacraments are considered in this way it becomes clear that there is no opposition between them and a completely moral interpretation of the scheme of salvation. Indeed they strengthen that view, because without a real desire and effort on our part to lead a good life they can be of no use to us. Further, the emphasis placed upon a right disposition and upon careful self-examination brings the need for moral goodness into strong relief, and makes the worshipper thoroughly conscious of the part he must play in his own salvation.

5

So far we have said little about the special importance of Ordination. Yet it is obvious that in any sacramental system it must occupy a foremost place, because the sacraments cannot be properly celebrated without a proper minister. It is true that in at least two cases, Baptism and Marriage, unordained people may occupy the place of a minister. In marriage the two partners make the necessary pledges to each other, and no one can do that for them. The grace of the sacrament depends upon their mutual consent. The priest acts as witness and gives the Church's blessing to the union. In the case of Baptism, it is regarded as so important for every human being to have the opportunity of entering the family of God during the course of his earthly life, that in the absence of the priest the rite may be performed by a lay person. But generally speaking the power to celebrate the sacraments is conferred on certain selected persons by ordination, and it is only those properly ordained who can minister valid sacraments on behalf of Christ.

The Church of England has always held that the three orders of Bishop, Priest and Deacon have come down to us from the Apostolic age, and it has attached great importance to the unbroken continuity of the ministry. Here again it is clear that if you accept the sacramental principle, then it is necessary to accept the need for proper authorization of those who are to minister the means of grace, and such authorization must link the Church of to-day with the Church of all the ages.

The method of that authorization is the laying on of hands with prayer by those ministers who are themselves given the right to ordain, namely the bishops. In this sense the bishops are the successors of the Apostles, and it is through them that the due succession of the Ministry has been preserved. The Church of England has no doubt at all that its own ministers are in that succession.

Unfortunately the Church of Rome does not accept that claim, but on what ground is not clear. Hitherto their theologians have contended that our Ordinations are invalid either because the 'instruments' of the Eucharist, that is chalice and paten, are not handed to the priest at his Ordination, or else because there is no avowed intent to ordain a priest at all. Recently, however, the Pope himself has laid it down that the laying on of the bishop's hands with an appropriate prayer constitutes the sufficient matter and form of the rite. The intention to ordain priests is made clear over and over again in the Anglican Ordinal.[1] The two main objections of Roman apologists seem therefore to have disappeared. There are, it is true, less worthy objections sometimes alleged, but as they appear to have been generally abandoned by Roman Catholic theologians they need not concern us here. One suspects that their real objection to our orders is that they are not given under Papal authority. The fact thus remains that the Church of England has a duly authorized ministry, deriving its orders in due succession from the primitive Church. It may therefore (granted also of course that it holds the

[1] Apart from the reiterated use of the name see especially the Preface to the Ordinal and the first rubric in the form for the Ordering of Priests. Note also the formula of ordination.

historic faith[1]) claim to be a part of the historic Church and to share whatever authority the Church has possessed from the beginning.

That authority we may here notice is the authority of the Holy Spirit working in and through the Church, which is the chosen instrument of God and the Body of Christ. When the first Christian Council met at Jerusalem, as described in the fifteenth chapter of the Acts of the Apostles, it concluded its proceedings by sending out an encyclical letter to the local churches. In that document it prefaced its decisions by saying, 'It has seemed good to the Holy Spirit and to us.' It is under that same Holy Spirit that the Church still claims to exercise its authority. The Spirit of God still moves and works in the Church to-day in accordance with the promise of Christ, 'I will send you another Comforter.' When Christ told His Apostles, 'Whatsoever ye shall bind on earth shall be bound in Heaven and whatsoever ye shall loose on earth shall be loosed in Heaven,' He was using a common idiom to say that the arrangements made by them were to be regarded as authoritative. We may therefore believe that when to-day ministers are acting in accordance with the express mind of the Church they are fulfilling the terms of this charter, and that for the purposes of human life upon this earth the authority of Heaven sanctions their ministrations.

It is important to recognize this participation of the whole Church in ministerial action because it is sometimes believed that individual members of the clergy, having once received a valid ordination, have *carte blanche* to do what they like. This is certainly not the case. A minister duly ordained must still act within the authority of the Church. When he has been ordained, although he has

[1] See Article XIX.

the power to minister valid sacraments, he still has no authority to do so until he has received the licence of his bishop. It is under that licence that he proceeds to fulfil proper functions, and it is that which gives him authority to act in the particular locality to which he is sent. That is what is meant by drawing a distinction between 'valid' and 'regular' ministrations. The sacraments ministered by a duly ordained person may be valid, that is to say, capable of conveying the promised grace, but they are not regular unless they are performed under proper ecclesiastical authority. When both conditions are fulfilled the faithful can be assured that the ministrations they receive are duly authorized. They themselves are living under authority and within the covenanted sphere of grace.

6

We cannot leave the consideration of the sacraments without recognizing how important and far-reaching is the principle involved. Without the sacraments we should experience an ever-widening gulf between the material and the spiritual. There would be no obvious contact between earth and heaven. Once on the first Christmas Day that contact was made clear in the birth of Christ. The doctrine of the Incarnation still reminds us that God is not far removed from the world of His creation. He did not make it of some alien material, and then retreat from it, and leave it to function alone. He is not only the Creator, but the Sustainer of the universe. The laws of nature are but the expression of His Will, and the planets in their courses are maintained by His power. As He may be said to have limited Himself by the very fact of a finite creation, so He entered into that creation in a special way when His eternal Word took human nature and was born of the Virgin Mary.

The redeeming contact of earth with heaven thus established and reinforced has never ceased. The sacraments are the extension of the Incarnation, a continued bestowal of the Incarnate Christ through specified material means. Thus sacraments stand as a continual witness to the fact that God's in His world. What we believe specifically of the sacraments we can see vaguely in other elements of the natural world. The God who can impart to His children the person of His Incarnate Son through the consecrated Bread and Wine displays the beauty of His presence in the ripening corn and the purpling grape. The sacraments are a standing witness to the spiritual constitution of the universe. Relying upon them it is easy for us to recognize that 'earth's crammed with Heaven and every common bush afire with God.'

CHAPTER VII

THE RULE OF WORSHIP

I

WE must now consider what the Church of England has to say to its members about worship. Inevitably the public meetings of God's family for common worship must be regulated with even more care than other elements of its common life. If the chief end of man is to glorify God, then the purpose of his being is expressed most adequately in worship, which is an activity directed specifically to God. It is well known how insistently St. Paul demands that everything connected with the worship of God shall be done without confusion and in proper order.[1] As far as the Church of England is concerned that order is laid down in the Book of Common Prayer.

The light in which the Church regards its handbook is stated quite clearly on the title page, which begins, 'The Book of Common Prayer and Administration of the Sacraments and Other Rites and Ceremonies of the Church according to the use of the Church of England.' This means that what is to be found here is the historic worship of the Church adapted for the use of this country. Behind the local church there lies the Great Church. There is no intention to depart from the ancient practices but merely to adapt them in a manner appropriate to our own needs. It was obviously intended to say in the plainest possible terms that in making this adaptation

[1] See especially 1 Cor. x–xiv.

the Church of England regarded itself as being a part of a greater whole. There can be no doubt about this intention because the phrase 'of the Church' was actually omitted in the 1552 revision of the Prayer Book when an effort was being made to change English services in response to the suggestions of Continental reformers, but in full view of the discussions that had occurred and with full knowledge of what the phrase implied it was actually restored in 1559 and has remained ever since. Therefore the general scheme of public worship and sacraments comes to us with the authority not only of the national, but of the universal Church.

We have already seen how this view is exemplified in the rule of belief as displayed in the creeds and articles. We have also had reason to emphasize it in the case of the sacraments and particularly of Ordination. The Ordinal indeed is not, strictly speaking, a part of the Prayer Book. It was originally issued separately, but it is now generally bound up with the Book of Common Prayer and is treated as having the same authority. In the next chapter we shall have to see how the same view is held with regard to the general tradition of Church teaching and doctrine as revealed in the Catechism. There, too, we have the Apostolic teaching handed down through the historic Church and reduced to a simple form for the instruction of English people. For the moment, however, we confine ourselves to the rule of worship.

The manner in which the Church in this country set itself to adapt the great classical traditions of worship for English use is set out in the Prefaces to the Book of Common Prayer. They are well worth studying and might with benefit be read over and over again by worshippers who find themselves in church waiting with some time on their hands for a service to begin. It should be realized that the first English Prayer Book was a product of the Reformation, drawn up by Cranmer and his advisers, and first authorized for use under King Edward VI in 1549. The compilers did not adopt the attitude of the Continental reformers, and of some leaders in this country, who wished to ignore the history of the Church and go right back to scriptural examples, making a completely fresh start with everything as they believed it to be practised in New Testament times. On the contrary they recognized the importance of the early fathers, and they called them as witnesses for the tradition they endeavoured to preserve in their own compilation. The bulk of the Book is therefore a translation of earlier forms, and where new additions are made there is an obvious and on the whole successful effort to follow historic models.

The compilers, however, were quite clear that many abuses had crept into the public worship of the later mediæval period, and they tried to get rid of them in drawing up the English book. The aims they had before them can be enumerated as follows: First, they wished to enable people to worship in their own language. The use of Latin was no longer deemed appropriate because it was understood only by a small minority. The new book is therefore in English throughout, although permission is expressly given for people to worship in other languages where they understand them. Secondly, the new Book is intended to establish one uniform use throughout the country. Hitherto each diocese had had its own use, the models being taken from the great cathedrals, of which Salisbury especially had a wide influence. No doubt those uses were closely similar to each other, yet there was enough difference to cause confusion. In a time of rapid change it was especially important to have one authoritative form of worship throughout the whole country. Thirdly, the new use was to be simple. An effort was made to get rid of many of the old elaborations and complications. Since the intention was to get the whole congregation to follow the services intelligently and to join together in repeating the people's part, it must be made easily possible for them to know what was going on and to turn up the changeable sections without undue delay. Fourthly, the new Book was to be made profoundly Biblical. Much more of the Bible was to be read, particularly in the choir offices, than had been customary in the immediate past. This was believed to be a return to early custom. Fifthly, as has already been pointed out, the intention was to preserve and popularize the old services. The Book was essentially Catholic, and indeed on this ground was objected to by the more extreme reformers. By a stroke of genius the old choir offices were combined into two, Mattins and Evensong, which were made of such full and yet simple structure that they could be found satisfying by educated people while still being capable of comprehension by the simple and unlearned. Lastly, the Book was intended to be 'reformed,' that is to say, it was to reflect the new emphasis of the reformed religion. As a revision of the ancient services it was itself the product of the Reformation, though of the English Reformation, which was quite unlike the Reformation in any other part of Europe. A later effort indeed was made, as we have seen, to assimilate it to the Continental Reformation, but this failed; and the Book remains, after its various revisions, as it began, typical of England and the part that England played in the religious changes.

As thus compiled the Book was imposed upon the country by Act of Parliament. An Act of Uniformity accompanied each revision. In the early revisions there was no corresponding Act of Convocation, but in the last important revision, that of 1662, the Book in its latest form was officially accepted by Convocation and thus the express authorization of the Church was added to that of Crown and Parliament. Thus the Book of 1662, which is in effect the Book as we have it to-day, has received full authorization both ecclesiastical and secular.

2

The Book of Common Prayer thus gives us our rule of public worship. It may, of course, be asked why we should be given such a book to guide our devotions and not be left to our own devices. The answer is that there must be some sort of direction when a number of people meet together with a common object, or else everything falls into confusion and the essential purpose is unlikely to be attained. St. Paul had to deal with this situation in Corinth, where there was a very enthusiastic spirit often finding expression in ecstatic utterances. The Apostle had to insist that no more than one person should be allowed to speak at once. Similarly in regulating the celebration of the Eucharist he had to remedy the confusion into which the Corinthians had fallen by reminding them of the exact words and actions of our Lord. It is not difficult to see how, in further efforts to produce order, stereotyped forms began to take the place of extemporaneous utterances, and to be regularly used in different parts of the Church. A precedent for such a development had already been set in contemporary Judaism. Scholars are generally agreed that a number of forms were taken over from Jewish models, and that the worship in the early Christian churches was to a large extent fashioned upon the worship of the synagogue.

But it might be asked, why, granted that there must be some direction, could it not be given in general terms, leaving the conductor to fill in the outline scheme according to the inspiration of the moment. A Directory was indeed substituted for the Book of Common Prayer under Presbyterian influence in 1645. Something of the same kind was proposed in the 1662 revision of the Prayer Book, when an effort was being made to reconcile the Puritans to the worship of the Church. Baxter, who was one of the ablest and most saintly of their leaders, proposed again to replace the Prayer Book with a Directory. The Anglican leaders, however, refused to accept this solution. To have adopted it would have been to depart from the custom of the ancient Church. After all, experience must count for something, and if Christian people had been led to retain these rites as the best means of expressing their common aspirations when engaged in the solemn worship of God, it was at least probable that they had found a system much more conducive to common devotion than that of leaving everything to the inspiration of the conductor. Their knowledge of the confusion produced when fixed forms were not used did not encourage them to accept Baxter's proposal. During the Commonwealth the Prayer Book had actually been banished for a considerable period, and the nation had had plenty of opportunity to learn what worship was like when it was divorced from the old and well-tried forms. They had no wish to renew such experiments. They preferred to remain in the old ways.

Much the same must be said with regard to the ceremonies employed. Churchmen were not prepared to abolish all ceremonial, as the Puritans would have wished. They acknowledged that ceremonies had been unnecessarily multiplied and had become difficult for

simple folk to follow. It has even to be acknowledged
that some had generated superstition. Nevertheless they
felt that certain ceremonies must be retained 'as well for
a decent order in the church as because they pertained to
edification.' They did not wish to condemn other people
who might prefer a still simpler form of service, but they
were very confident that what they had arranged was
suitable to English people at that time and was likely to
prove acceptable to them. 'In these our doings we
condemn no other nation, nor prescribe anything but
to our own people only; for we think it convenient that
every country should use such ceremonies as they shall
think best to the setting forth of God's honour and glory,
and to the reducing of the people to a most perfect and
Godly living, without error or superstition.'

Consequently the new order continued to follow the
well established system of the Church's year. The
compilers had no desire, as had some of the reformers,
to dispense even with the great festivals of Christmas and
Easter. The value of such commemorations having been
accepted it was obvious that other feasts and fasts should
be recognized as well. They served a double purpose.
They enabled the worshipper to keep in constant touch
with the historical life of Christ and the great topics of
Christian doctrine. They also incorporated variety into
what otherwise might have been too uniform and monoto-
nous an observance. The fact that to-day most of the
descendants of the Puritan teachers themselves observe
the main variations of the Church's year shows how wise
were the compilers in their decision.

One of the most valuable consequences of this arrange-
ment was that it enabled the compilers to make special
provision for every day. Although the number of
variations in the Eucharistic liturgy was considerably

reduced, yet the choir office, beside its fixed portion, had variations for each morning and evening throughout the year. The daily recitation of the Psalms follows a monthly course, and the readings from the Bible an annual course. All the clergy were bound to use this regularly, and the laity were expected to share in it when they had suitable opportunity. 'All Priests and Deacons are to say daily the Morning and Evening Prayer either privately or openly, not being let by sickness or some other urgent cause. And the curate that ministereth in every parish church or chapel, and not being otherwise reasonably hindered shall say the same in the parish church or chapel where he ministereth and shall cause a bell to be tolled thereunto a convenient time before he begin that the people may come to hear God's Word and to pray with him.'

3

In addition to this order for common worship the Prayer Book provides for more personal ministrations. What are known as the occasional services are forms for individual worship, sometimes in public and sometimes in private. They show that the Church has a regard not only for the whole family of God, but also for each several member. Every opportunity is taken to relate the life of each person to his religion, and to encourage him to seek the help and blessing of God at every turning point in his existence. Thus we have services for Baptism, Confirmation, Marriage, Thanksgiving after Childbirth, Sickness, and Burial. There is no occasion when the Church does not care for her children. No opportunity is lost in bringing them into immediate contact with God.

These personal ministrations are perhaps the occasions on which the average man finds the Church touching him most nearly. We have already noticed how many people bring their children to be baptized, even when they have no very close connection with the Church. However indifferent they are, most of them turn to God for help and comfort in bereavement, and few of them wish to enter upon married life without the public pronouncement of God's blessing upon their union. This is shown even when a first marriage has broken down. In days when there is a widespread departure from the Christian rule of marriage, it is pathetic to realize how many divorcees believe that their own case is exceptional, and crave the Church's help and blessing in making the best of a new partnership into which, with the aid of the State, they are about to launch themselves. The Church is prepared to help its members to the utmost in all circumstances, but it cannot presume to marry a divorced person whose original spouse is still living. Its steadfast witness in this respect has done much to preserve the stability of family life and indeed of the whole social structure of the country.

It is perhaps also in these occasional services that we find religion, as formally expressed in the rites of the Church, penetrating most deeply into the conscience of the people. The service for the visitation of the sick, for instance, where its intentions are still followed, encourages the seriously ill to set their house in order and, as far as possible, to make provision for those they may leave behind. Further, it makes abundantly clear a man's duty to meet his God with a clean conscience. He must see to it that on entering the divine presence he is conscious of no unrepented sin, and that before he confronts the divine holiness he has humbly accepted that redemption which the Saviour of mankind gave His life to procure for him.

4

Inevitably the greater part of the Prayer Book is concerned with the observances of Sunday. No Christian can feel himself free to give himself up entirely to secular affairs on the Lord's Day. If his twofold nature, as a spiritual as well as a material being, is to be adequately developed, he must remind himself from time to time what is due to his spiritual needs. Time is essential for such recognition, and one day in the week must be set apart as a special opportunity for recollection. But quite apart from man's own needs there is the overwhelming claim of God upon his attention. A father has a right to expect some consideration from his children, and no child can, without incurring the danger of ingratitude, absent himself entirely from the normal gatherings of the family. It was one of the earliest acts of the Christian Church to set apart the first day of each week for such meetings of those who shared in the sonship of Christ.

For the Sunday, therefore, the Prayer Book makes special provision. There is not only the usual daily round of the Christian offices, but there is also a special liturgy for each Lord's day. The original intention of the Book was that Mattins and Litany should be a preparation for the celebration of the Eucharist. The Eucharist was always intended to be the main gathering for Christian worship, 'the Lord's own service on the Lord's own day.' The weekly commemoration of Christ's resurrection was observed by the repetition of the rite He Himself had celebrated with His disciples before He suffered. This was the rule until comparatively recent times. It was a quite unauthorized departure from the original form when the central part of the Liturgy began to be omitted and people were content first with a truncated form of the

Eucharist and then with its omission altogether. That abuse happily never became universal, and now it is extremely uncommon. What has happened to-day is that the services have been separated from each other, and their order treated as variable.

To-day there is, perhaps, no greater necessity in the life of the Church than a fresh insistence upon the obligation resting upon each member of the Christian family to be present at least once every Lord's day at public worship. The sense of that obligation will be most easily restored if people are taught the supreme importance of the Eucharist. This is specifically Christian worship. Nothing can properly take its place. Happily that fact is rapidly becoming more generally recognized among Christians of almost every type.

It is, perhaps, our variations in this respect which more than anything else lead to the charge that there is no authority in the Church of England. Worship, although it is based on the Prayer Book, is nevertheless presented in very different forms. The outstanding difficulty is that people who are accustomed to go to church at 11.0 on a Sunday morning are not certain what service they will find, whether Morning Prayer or the Eucharist. Even if it is the latter, it may vary in kind from a Choral Communion to a full High Mass. This variety is sometimes contrasted both by our critics and by our own people with the worship of other parts of Christendom where, it is said, everyone knows exactly what to expect. Whether such hard and fast identity is altogether an advantage may be doubted. It is, perhaps, the earlier insistence on uniformity, under Acts of Parliament which were promulgated rather for political than for ecclesiastical reasons, that has made us feel that any departure from a fixed norm is to be deprecated. It may be suggested, however, that it was probably never intended that services should always be conducted in precisely the same way. The distinction between a plain and a sung service is, perhaps, the most obvious difference. There are, of course, many people who never join in public worship except on a Sunday and who have never heard a public service without music. In the same way there are some who have never attended Morning or Evening Prayer, and others who find themselves lost in the ceremonies of the Eucharist. No one of these should claim the right to regard his own custom as the only legitimate one.

In any case it may be said that the breakdown of uniformity is much more obvious than the breakdown of authority. It is not at all certain on what ground rigid uniformity is ever demanded. The Preface says: 'It hath been the wisdom of the Church of England, ever since the first compiling of her public Liturgy, to keep the mean between the two extremes, of too much stiffness in refusing, and of too much easiness in admitting any variation from it.' The question is rather to what extent variation may be allowed. That some variation is not only inevitable but valuable will probably be admitted by anyone who is not bound by prejudice. One remedy for the present distress would be to see that worshippers are trained in different types of service so that they never feel completely strange whatever church they enter. It would surely be reasonable to expect Church people to know the whole of their Prayer Book and not merely one part of it. And probably their religious experience would be greatly enriched if they could appreciate various interpretations of its worship. Certainly the average bishop whose work takes him into every kind of church and to every kind of service finds it difficult to understand those who clamour for an entirely monochrome presentation of Prayer Book services.

It might be easier to say how far variation should be allowed if we could fix precisely the nature of the dispensing power. The priest at his Ordination and at other times has to promise that he will use the services provided in the Prayer Book and none other except as shall be ordered by lawful authority. Our real difficulty is to decide what in this context is the meaning of 'lawful authority.' To some it is a vague custom which they identify as Catholic use. To others it is to be found in the judgements of the Judicial Committee of the Privy Council. To others it is just the Prayer Book as they interpret it themselves. To others again it is the voice of their diocesan bishop. An effort is at present being made to define lawful authority in a new canon. It is expected that if a definition can be found and generally accepted we shall be able to satisfy consciences that are disturbed by the present varieties in worship. It is to be hoped that we shall not endeavour to rule out varieties altogether. We may indeed find it necessary to check the idiosyncrasies of incumbents who describe as 'days of obligation' feasts that have never been recognized by the Church of England at all, and of others who before administering the Holy Communion invite all and sundry of whatever denomination to come and 'partake.' But such oddities apart, there should be left sufficient room for agreed differences and improvements.

A major difficulty is that at the moment we are faced with two contrary needs. The one is for greater simplicity and the other for greater elaboration. As for the first, we need to-day the kind of simplicity which would make our services intelligible to people who come to them for the first time. The worshipping Church is a comparatively small body. It is handicapped when it tries to draw the multitude to its services by the fact that the language used and the ceremonies employed are only thoroughly understood by those who through long experience have become experts. On the other hand, for those who have become experts we need considerably more elaboration than is at present provided. The practice of frequent Communion has grown tremendously in modern times, and there is a quite considerable number of Church members who attend the Eucharist daily. For them something more is needed than distinctive services for Sundays and holy days. Some variation in the Liturgy parallel to that provided in the choir office, is needed for the other days of the week.

How we are to reconcile these apparently opposed needs is not at present clear. To some extent we meet the first need on days of great national sorrow or rejoicing by issuing a special service which is printed on an occasional sheet so that each worshipper may have it in his hand. The other need is partially met by incorporating into the Eucharist special Collects, Epistles, and Gospels for many saints' days. But it is obvious both that our calendar needs a good deal of revision and that there must be suitable services for the new observances when they are arranged. But this need give no concern to the faithful worshipper. The Prayer Book is made for man and not man for the Prayer Book. Our liturgical standards, splendid as they are, have not yet reached perfection. Religion is life, and when life ceases to develop it dies.

CHAPTER VIII

THE RULE OF FAITH

I

'ONE generation to another.' It must be the proudest privilege of any generation to hand on to its successor the stored-up wisdom, which it has inherited and to which it has been able to add its own experience. Every parent wishes to hoist his child on to his shoulders to give it a better view of its surroundings and a greater opportunity of mounting the heights he himself has been unable to reach. Normally we expect this duty to be shared by our educational institutions. It is for this reason that many who have been blessed with this world's goods have gladly seized the opportunity to improve our equipment of schools and colleges.

A few years ago a French writer fluttered the educational dovecotes by roundly accusing the universities of misconceiving their specific duty. They had contented themselves with imparting scientific and technical skill, and they had failed altogether to give to their pupils any practical philosophy of life. They seemed, he alleged, to have no adequate view either of the purpose for which a university exists or of the best way to fit the individual to it. To such a charge it was always possible for the universities to reply, rightly or wrongly, that the moral training of the students was not their especial concern. That, said some at least of their defenders, was the duty of the Church. Certainly, whatever we may think of the universities, we shall be very ready to accept a share of the responsibility on behalf of the Church. If the Church exists, as we have so often contended, to carry on the work of Christ, then it must regard it as a primary duty to hand on His interpretation of life and to assist all and sundry to avail themselves of His revelation.

From the beginning the Church recognized this duty. It fulfilled it in two ways, by preaching and by teaching. The preaching took the form of an effort to win converts by the proclamation to the world of the good news of the salvation brought by Christ. That was always the first and most necessary step. The teaching, by contrast, was the development of Christian doctrine on a broader basis, with the purpose of edification rather than conversion, aiming at the intellect rather than the will. Inevitably such teaching, of which there is abundant evidence in the New Testament, would tend to become systematized. Not all the teachers would present precisely the same scheme of salvation with an equal emphasis upon the same details. Nevertheless in broad outline it would remain identical. Modern scholarship has taught us to appreciate the variety of presentation that can be discerned in different New Testament writers; but the main lines of Christian doctrine remain the same in them all.

This teaching in its most condensed form was given in the creeds. But side by side with the creeds, and indeed forming a general background to them, was a 'rule of faith' which covered far more ground and went into much greater detail. This rule of faith has recently been defined as an 'outline summary of Christian teaching, used for ethical instruction and other purposes.'[1] Such instruction would be imparted to candidates for baptism in days when that sacrament was normally confined to adults. The creeds, as the most concise form of this teaching, would be

[1] J. N. D. Kelly, *Early Church Creeds*, p. 2.

learned by heart, but they would have been almost incomprehensible without the careful instruction in the rule of faith which went along with them.

The Church of England remains true to this age-long custom. In its Prayer Book it gives us not only the creeds, but also the rule of faith. This is to be found in the Catechism. It even retains the old method of instruction as well as its substance. The Catechism, as the name properly implies, is built on the lines of oral question and answer.

2

From our present point of view the Catechism represents the hard core of the Book of Common Prayer. We can learn there as well as anywhere what the Church of England stands for. The fact that it is intended primarily for children and young people preparing for Confirmation means that its teaching is given in a simple and direct manner. The fact that, unlike the Articles, it has no direct reference to contemporary controversies means that it is less 'dated' and more balanced in its judgement. Therefore within its limited sphere it gives a better idea of Church teaching as a whole than any other section of the Book.

Its history is interesting. It represents a sixteenth-century return to early models. The fashion of catechetical instruction had been considerably modified during the late Middle Ages. Priests had been expected to instruct the young in the Lord's Prayer, the Creed, and the Ten Commandments. Manuals of instruction on these subjects had been issued, but they were intended for the use of the clergy rather than to be put into the hands of the catechumens. At the time of the Reformation, when efforts were being made to remedy the comparative

G

ignorance of the laity about religious matters, the method of instruction by question and answer, involving on the part of the pupil the learning by heart of prescribed answers, came once again into vogue. The Anglican Catechism followed these lines, basing itself upon the three necessary points of erudition for every Christian man, the Lord's Prayer, the Creed, and the Ten Commandments, but prefacing them by an introduction on the baptismal covenant. This was included in the 1549 Book as part of the Service of Confirmation, candidates being expected to answer the questions before the Confirmation prayer proceeded.

Later, owing to criticism by the Puritans, there seemed likely to be a proposal for a much longer and more prolix production. The proposal was forestalled by the suggestion that the need might be sufficiently met if a section were added on the Sacraments. A fuller Catechism by Dr. Nowell, Dean of St. Paul's, for adults had indeed been published, although it never found its way into the Prayer Book. When Dr. Overall, then Dean of St. Paul's, was asked to prepare a section on the Sacraments he returned to this fuller Catechism of Dr. Nowell and based his own appendix on it. This was added to the existing Prayer Book by Royal authority in 1604 and with a couple of small emendations was confirmed by the Convocations and Parliament in 1662. Thus, like the rest of the 1662 Book, it comes to us with the fullest authorization it could have from both Church and State.

3

The contents of the Catechism as it now exists fall into five parts. The first deals with baptism, and makes clear the individual's own part in the scheme of redemption.

It emphasizes the privileges he enjoys as 'a member of Christ, the child of God and an inheritor of the Kingdom of Heaven.' It affirms that he has been chosen out of the world in accordance with God's normal method of selection and has been placed in a special relationship to Christ, and that he already, living as he does on this high plane of existence, enjoys a foretaste of the final glory that will be his in Heaven. The section also makes it clear that these privileges bring responsibilities, and that as a child of God the baptized member must behave as befits the family. He must set himself to fight against all that is evil both in himself and in the world. As a believing Christian, he must display those moral qualities which are enjoined in God's commandments.

The second section repeats the Apostles' Creed and explains it in the clearest way by emphasizing the three articles upon which it is based: 'God the Father, who hath made me and all the world; God the Son, who hath redeemed me and all mankind; and God the Holy Ghost, who sanctifieth me and all the elect people of God.'

The third section deals with the Ten Commandments and explains them in the 'duty towards God' and 'duty towards one's neighbour.' With the latter we shall have to deal in another chapter. The former is an admirable summary of the attitude which should be displayed by the believing soul towards its Maker. It stresses the fact that true religion is not some lukewarm tolerance of a spiritual status, but a wholehearted love of God expressing itself in worship, thankfulness and complete trust. It is thus an attitude of the whole personality towards its Creator and Redeemer. This love of the soul for God is the most important aspect of our relationship to that total existence of which in virtue of our birth we find ourselves a part.

The fourth section begins with the assertion that we cannot live on this high level by any strength of our own, but only through the special grace of God. For that grace we have been taught to pray by our Lord Himself. There follows the Lord's Prayer with the explanation of it in the answer generally known as the Desire. The Desire follows each phrase of the Lord's Prayer and brings out its meaning, emphasizing the fact that we pray to God not only for spiritual but for material blessings as they may be needful for us. The phrase which is sometimes found difficult, 'Lead us not into temptation,' is explained as meaning 'that it will please Him to save us in all dangers ghostly and bodily,' while 'Deliver us from evil' is expanded into the request that He will 'keep us from all sin and wickedness and from our ghostly enemy and from everlasting death.' It would be very difficult to give a more adequate or concise paraphrase of the model prayer.

The appendix on the Sacraments confines itself to the two Sacraments which are 'generally,' that is universally, necessary to salvation, Baptism and the Supper of the Lord. We have already seen that the explanation of the character of sacraments makes it clear that they are not mere symbols, but actual means by which grace is given. The outward sign and the inward grace are carefully distinguished, but the duality is accepted as essential for every sacrament. Emphasis is also laid upon the disposition with which the sacraments should be received if they are to be effective, and no room is left for any magical or superstitious use. The whole section is thoroughly religious and can stand the test of the most rigorous theological examination.

4

It is not difficult to see what scheme of salvation lies behind this Catechism. It presupposes an eternal sphere in which dwells the threefold personality of the God-head. In God's original intention for the universe human spirits were created 'after His own likeness' in such a sense that they would be able to enjoy with Him His own infinitude of bliss. Foreseeing, however, that man would use his freedom to rebel against his Creator and follow his own selfish purposes, God made the universe of such a kind as to serve as a school of training and correction. We therefore at our birth are introduced to a world of mingled good and evil, which, precisely because of its double character, is a suitable training ground for the human soul. The individual, awakening to self-conscious-ness, finds himself the denizen of two spheres and must choose either to yield supinely to the lower elements or to strive manfully to follow the dictates of the higher.

God who has thus created man does not leave him alone in his struggles, but has planted a certain knowledge of Himself in every man's heart. When this proved insuffi-cient He showed His purpose more clearly by His selection of the chosen people, to whom He revealed His nature more fully and taught them the code of conduct that would be pleasing to Him. He sent His prophets to warn His people never to depart from His ways, and to look forward to a complete and final revelation of Himself. Only a few, however, lived in accordance with His law, and when in the person of the Messiah the ultimate revelation was vouchsafed, only a remnant even of the chosen people accepted it.

The Christ came not only to complete the revelation of God, but also to redeem men from the sin into which they had fallen. He was God Incarnate, not only Jesus the prophet of Nazareth, but also the embodiment of God's eternal Word. As archetypal man He yielded Himself voluntarily to the death which resulted from His fellow-men's rejection of Him. He not only paid the penalty for their sin, but by the preservation of His own innocence broke the power of sin. Henceforth all who attached themselves to Him would be free both from the power of sin and from its penalties. The true character of the Messiah was made clear to those who believed in Him by His Resurrection from the tomb. The association between Christ and the believers is far closer than that between God and His people under the old dispensation. By baptism they are united with Christ in such a way that they die with Him in His death to sin and rise again with Him to the new life of righteousness. To them is therefore granted the power of an endless life.

Thus a new Israel was spiritually constituted to take the place of the chosen people of old. This new selection is identified with the Church. It is no longer national, but includes people of every race and clime. The oneness with Christ is secured not altogether by faith in Him, but also by the sacraments, which not only symbolically represent, but actually cement that union. In all this is to be seen the work of the Holy Spirit, who applies the life of Christ to men and leads them to that ideal character which makes them more and more like Him to whom they are being conformed.

It should be noticed that this scheme of salvation embodies an appeal to different sides of human nature. It applies to both mind and soul. It demands faith and it assumes the sacraments. It is intellectual and vital. It has a psychological and also an ontological aspect. In accordance with it men are expected not only to draw up their will in line with that of Christ, but actually to share in His life. They are to have complete trust in Him, accepting their salvation as a free gift, and at the same time they are to be made partakers of the divine nature, imbibing it, so to speak, by frequent participation in the sacraments and giving it exercise and expression by every effort after conformity to the will of Christ.

Also it can be seen that with its strong emphasis upon the Ten Commandments and one's duty towards one's neighbour the Catechism is thoroughly moralistic. It is not merely emotional or formal. Still less is it magical. It stresses the necessity of good moral living. In a characteristically English way it gives much space to the moral aspect of the Christian life. Faith, sacraments and ethics are not three distinct and separable elements of the Christian life. They are all part and parcel of the same scheme of redemption.

5

It is certainly high time that in our schools of instruction we inaugurated a return to the Catechism. For too long its value has been discounted, not on any religious ground, but on the plea that it is not suitable for modern methods of teaching. The habit of making children learn by heart answers to stereotyped questions is supposed by many to develop memory at the expense of thought. However, a reaction has recently taken place among educationists. It is now generally agreed that it is valuable for us all to know by heart a summary of what we have been taught at length. The reasoning faculties may be extended to the full before the child is asked finally to grasp a succinct statement and to repeat it by heart. There is no necessary conflict between memory and thought; they should normally assist each other.

Another reason why the time is ripe for a return to the Catechism is the modern departure from Christian standards of conduct. We are not without cause for distress at the extent of youthful delinquency and at the increase in crimes of violence and in the general decay of honesty at all ages. There are many contributory causes for this moral decline. At least one of them is that children are not so carefully taught the fundamental truths of religion as they used to be. With the new Education Acts now in force it is hoped that there will be a general improvement in this respect. All children must now receive some instruction in the rudiments of faith and worship unless their parents deliberately and formally object. In the course of that improvement we may well hope that there will be a considerable revival of interest in the Catechism. Its strong moralistic tone combined with its careful basing of the moral law on religious principles, and its clear indication where spiritual power can be found should give us just what is needed at the present juncture. It was perhaps symptomatic of this view that an Australian Primate was heard to say that half the moral difficulties in that country would be met if only the Duty to My Neighbour were posted on the walls of every classroom in the land.

It is sometimes objected that the Catechism speaks too much of the fear of God and assumes too easily the old-fashioned sanction of rewards and punishments. It may be questioned, however, whether this is in itself wholly bad. To eliminate the idea of rewards and punishment altogether from religious teaching would be to remove a powerful incentive which our Lord Himself did not hesitate to employ. No doubt what we all wish to aim at in the long run is a pure and disinterested love. But that is probably seldom reached except by the most devoted mothers and the most advanced saints. There is at the other end of the scale a considerable body of people who may be kept from doing wrong by the fear of punishment. It is well for us all to know that the way of transgressors is hard. We are doing an injustice to the rising generation if we allow them to feel that the way of death may be just as pleasant and rewarding as the way of life. As someone has pointed out, rewards and punishments, love and discipline, are not mutually exclusive. We learn even as children to recognize the sanity of parents who punish us if we deliberately run risks and incur danger. We know, as we look back, that but for their discipline our life and health might not have been preserved at all. If the Catechism warns us of possible dangers and of a punishment that may ensue upon wrongdoing, it is following the natural as well as the divine law, and it may lead us to appreciate the protective care of the Creator who has fashioned His universe in such a way as to provide a corrective for human frailty and sin.

CHAPTER IX

THE RULE OF CONDUCT

I

EVERYONE wishes to know how to behave in society. Most people, if they have an inquiring turn of mind, are anxious to go further and to know what are the fundamental principles that should dictate their attitude to the world in which they live. Certainly English people have always shown a special interest in questions of practical conduct. Even in the sphere of philosophy it has been in the section devoted to morals and ethics that English thinkers have been most conspicuous. In the sphere of theology it is interesting that the only major heresy which has emanated from these islands concerned itself with problems relating to the nature of man and his capacity for goodness.

Obviously it is inevitable that the Church should be expected to give authoritative guidance on matters of this kind. People want to know what their relations should be with their fellow men. They have a duty not only towards God, but also towards men. The difficulty of adjusting oneself to society presses on us from the cradle to the grave.

This is the kind of problem which admits no easy solution. Life is more than logic and human beings are often said to be unaccountable. One cannot foresee with mathematical certitude how anyone will act in any given circumstances. As this uncertainty applies both to oneself and also to the people with whom one has to do, the possible variety of personal situations is almost infinite. Each situation is fresh for each individual. 'We shall never pass this way again.' It is very necessary that some kind of compass should be provided for every voyager through these unexplored seas.

The interest of the Bible in such questions is, of course, profound. It is revealed on every page. The Old Testament is not interested in purely metaphysical questions. It reveals God as one who acts, and it is to action, whether divine or human, that it gives its closest attention. Its particular type of monotheism is often described as 'ethical' monotheism because it insists that God is good. By contrast the ancient Greeks and Romans had little interest in the moral character of their deities. Jehovah is singular in that He is revealed as 'holy,' not only in the sense that He is far above the world and its ways, but also because His very nature is righteousness.

As God is righteous it follows that those who would serve Him and try to please Him must endeavour to be righteous too. A very large part of the Old Testament is given up to the elucidation of the law which should govern men's relations with God and with each other. There is at first no hard and fast distinction between ritual and moral law. Nevertheless it is possible to trace a growing emphasis upon the unique character of moral acts. For a large part of their history the Hebrew people regarded themselves as a close-knit social unit. They were 'bound up in the same bundle of life together.' It was the solidarity of the race and its combined responsibility before God that was in the forefront. The whole nation rather than the single citizen was the subject of the moral code. With Jeremiah and Ezekiel there at last emerges a real emphasis upon the individual, and the single personality is seen both as a responsible agent before God and as a recipient of His rewards and punishments.

At what particular point in this development the Ten Commandments are to be placed is not clear. It is possible that in their complete form as found in Exodus xx they belong to the exilic period, but it is regarded as certain by modern scholars that they must have existed in simpler forms long before that. The very fact that they are so condensed, and that they are numbered for the fingers on each hand (so that they can easily be remembered) suggests a great antiquity. At any rate they embody the Law of the Jews in its most succinct form. It has been natural to recognize them as the simplest code of conduct to be learned and to be used as the foundation of all godly living.

Jewish interest in behaviour did not stop here, but was extended to cover all possible details of life in society. In the Wisdom literature such as Ecclesiastes and Proverbs, Wisdom and Ecclesiasticus, efforts were made to provide well-intentioned people with a guide in all questions of morals and manners and to warn the ill-intentioned of the danger of their ways.

2

When we come to the New Testament, we find that this interest is maintained and even increased. A new direction is given to it in the teaching of our Lord. He proclaimed that He had come to 'fulfil' the Law. His implied intention was not simply to repeat it in the precise form in which it was to be found in the Jewish scriptures, but to direct its development towards its proper end. He refrained, in a quite marked degree, from laying down new regulations, but He did disentangle principles and lay tremendous stress upon them. Thus He endorsed that summary of the law which emphasized its positive character rather than its negative prohibitions, by singling out the two principles of love to God and love to one's neighbour. Further, in the Beatitudes, He laid down what Seely has described as the 'new law' for His Kingdom, pronouncing His benediction on those virtues which befitted the fresh revelation He had given of God.

An individual turn was given to this discussion by St. Paul. He found that the whole conception of law had entered so deeply into the religious consciousness of his contemporaries that many, even after they had become Christians, continued to think that their hope of salvation depended upon the faithful fulfilment of its obligations. Logically this meant that people could earn their own redemption, an idea which was utterly abhorrent to St. Paul and seemed to him to conflict with the most fundamental elements of Christ's teaching. Salvation, St. Paul taught, could not be earned. It could only be accepted as a free gift from Christ. Christ had won freedom for us, and all we could do was humbly to stretch out our hand and accept it from Him. Psychologically this was of the utmost importance because it meant that humility and faith, not pride in one's own achievements, must be the essential characteristic of the man of God. This, of course, was the truth embodied in our Lord's parable of the Pharisee and the Publican. Of all His followers St. Paul saw it most clearly, and insisted most strongly upon its fundamental position in the Christian scheme of salvation.

There was some danger in this teaching. It was possible to say that if we could do nothing to earn our own salvation, then even the moral law was of no importance and the Christian need not bother about good works. There were some who fell into this error of antinomianism, and they were reproved by St. James in his Epistle.

He said that faith without works was dead, and he contended that a man's faith could be known only by his works. This was to some extent a correction of the Pauline teaching. It was not, however, opposed to it; it was merely complementary. St. Paul himself had rebutted the charge of those who said that he taught, 'Let us do evil that good may come.' That he was in fact not indifferent to good works is shown quite clearly in all his epistles, particularly in those which conclude with a moral code. Ephesians and Colossians, to say nothing of I Timothy and Titus, contain outline schemes which Luther called 'Tables of Manners,' showing what kind of conduct was appropriate for specific classes of society. Wives, husbands, children, fathers, slaves and masters, are all told how they should behave and what were the appropriate virtues of their condition or calling.

There is one difference between these Christian laws and the law of the Old Testament. In the Pauline codes the virtues are expected to be displayed 'in Christ.' In other words, they do not represent an external system of virtue, ideals to which one must be continually reaching out, but they are rather the natural expression of the inward life of Christ imparted to the believer. Thus in the Pauline system the virtues are of no value to gain us salvation; they are the normal sign of the saved life. This may be regarded as the proper distinction between the Christian rule of conduct and every legalistic system, whether Jewish or other.

3

We can now see with what kind of authority the Church speaks to us on this subject. It hands on to us the revelation it has received, that is, the revelation contained in the whole Bible. Too many people are inclined to stop at the

Old Testament and to forget the New. 'That is what I believe, Padre,' said an officer on active service, 'the good old Bible rule, an eye for an eye and a tooth for a tooth!' But that is *not* the Bible rule. It was the rule at a certain early stage of the development of the Jewish people, but it was a merely temporary part of their training. Christ carried the lesson to its completion when He said, 'Love your enemies, do good to them that hate you.' Christians learn to interpret the Old Testament by the New.

In other respects, also, Christ brought out the new principles of Christian conduct and showed how they re-interpreted and 'fulfilled' the old regulations. It is not only murder that is forbidden, but hatred; not only theft, but covetousness. Merely to avoid adultery was not sufficient to satisfy the demands of the Christian law: one must also avoid giving place to lustful thoughts.

In all this it was the *principle* upon which Christ laid emphasis. It is sometimes said that there was only one rule that He laid down with the force of a legal enactment and that was His prohibition of divorce. This is indeed so unique in the whole range of His teaching that some scholars have thought that it cannot actually have been done by Him. Others, however, with greater probability maintain that this departure from His usual custom shows the tremendous importance He attached to the institution of marriage.

In any case it is essential to notice that the New Testament does not set us to the task of 'acquiring merit,' much less does it lead us to think that on our success in that effort depends our hope of ultimate salvation. What it does is to show us how we can be united with Christ, and how, so long as that union holds, His virtues will manifest themselves in us.

4

It is in this spirit that the 'duty towards my neighbour' in the Catechism explains the Ten Commandments. We have seen that the Ten are divided into two parts, one devoted to our duty towards God and the other towards our neighbour, the one to piety and the other to probity. The first four commandments deal obviously with strictly religious matters. The fifth, bidding us honour our father and mother, seems to us moderns to belong more naturally to the second section dealing with social matters, but to the ancients duty towards parents seemed more obviously a branch of piety. Of the remaining five, the first three deal with actions, forbidding murder, adultery and theft. The ninth deals with words, 'Thou shalt not bear false witness against thy neighbour'; and the tenth deals with thoughts, prohibiting covetous desires. The last is unexpected in this context, but it shows that already ethical teachers had begun to realize that moral evil is not confined to the external act, but springs from the inner thoughts of the heart. Thus it already points the way towards the moral teaching of Christ.

The explanation of the latter section of the commandments found in the 'duty towards my neighbour' opens with the golden rule, 'My duty towards my neighbour is to love him as myself, and to do to all men as I would they should do unto me.' Most of us can remember how strangely it sounded in our ears when we first heard it as children. However well we had been brought up there was still enough of primitive instinct in the nursery to make us feel how foreign to our usual ways was the command to love our neighbour. But if that sounded vague enough to be ignored, the precision of 'to do to all men as I would they should do unto me' was too definite to be escaped. Only to do to others what you hoped they would do to you in similar circumstances did give a very definite standard by which to test your conduct. It could be taken as a touchstone by which to judge everything one did. In the 'duty towards my neighbour' it is intended to set the tone for the rest of the injunctions. Upon that rule depends our attitude to our parents, to all lawful authorities, and to those who have any claim upon our special respect.

'To order myself lowly and reverently to all my betters' may seem to have an old-world sound about it, but it is probably more necessary than ever in an age when we are inclined to lay stress upon the essential equality of every living person. There is, of course, no more than a formal opposition between a belief in such equality and a respectful attitude towards those in authority. This is clear in the teaching of Jesus. In the interview between our Lord and the centurion, the latter received a word of special praise because he had discerned that Christ recognized Himself as being *under* authority. The implication is that as the Son submits to the Father, so we should recognize the rights of those under whose direction we live and work. The centurion lived within a military system, and he knew that his only claim to obedience from others lay in the fact that he himself rendered obedience to higher authority. In every organized society, however far it may depart from military standards, essentially the same obligation must be recognized. The very idea of order implies a proper recognition of authority. That recognition must not be grudging, but willing and wholehearted; otherwise the wheels of the organization are bound to creak and groan, and there can be no smoothness of operation.

H

The injunctions 'To hurt nobody by word nor deed: To be true and just in all my dealing' are reinforced by the characteristic New Testament emphasis upon inner motive and disposition. We are to bear no malice nor hatred in our heart. Similarly the prohibition of the act of stealing is balanced by the prohibition of lying and slanderous words. It is St. James who in the New Testament gives the most homely warning against the wrong use of the tongue. 'How great a matter a little fire kindleth.' 'The tongue is a fire, a world of iniquity among our members . . . and is set on fire by hell.'

The seventh Commandment is interpreted as implying the need to keep one's body in 'temperance, soberness and chastity,' thus enlarging its scope to cover the steps that may lead to adultery. Finally, the tenth Commandment is interpreted not only to prohibit inordinate desire for other men's goods, but to give emphasis to the need for honest work and the earning of one's own living.

The whole explanation concludes with the instruction to do one's duty in that state of life to 'which it shall please God to call me.' It is unfortunate that so many interpreters in the past have failed to notice the future tense and have regarded the words as implying a wish to maintain a purely static condition of society. It is, perhaps, even more unfortunate that the mistake on this point has led to forgetfulness of the emphasis that is here laid upon God's calling. Here, if we had eyes to see, is an assertion that every man has his own vocation from God. God has a place for each one of us in His great scheme of things, and He calls upon us, each one, to fulfil our proper part. As we have already seen, there is no distinction in this respect between secular and religious. There is a vocation not only for the priesthood, but for every trade and profession. All of us should have our ears open to God's voice so that we may know to what work He summons us. This will be the best guarantee that we shall prove ourselves worthy of His calling, and face our duty without fear of failure.

5

It must be recognized that the teaching of the Catechism is in sharp contrast to much of the prevailing sentiment of our time. The modern ideologies have a quite different inspiration. Indeed, it would not be too much to say that most of them are derived from a complete reaction against the point of view here presented. Nietzsche thought this kind of sentiment fit only for slaves and the underdog. His complaint against Christianity was that it led men to submit too easily, and therefore to miss the opportunity to make the most of themselves. He wished to build up a race of superior quality, and said that that could only be done as we learnt to jettison the self-abasing virtues and in place of them put the motive of self-aggrandisement. If this set you at enmity with your neighbours, then you should be glad of the opportunity of sharpening your sword against them and finding in the conflict new strength and skill for the struggle on behalf of your own interests.

It is not to be wondered at that this kind of teaching developed into the totalitarian system of recent times. It is true that defenders of Nietzsche have asked how his sheer individualism could have been turned into the totalitarian creed. The answer is that the transition from the individual to the class, from the class to the nation, is quite easily made. What Nietzsche said of the necessity for a self-regarding policy on the part of the individual, other people have claimed to be necessary on the part of the class or the community. When you add to this the

H*

modern 'leadership principle,' it is still easier to see how the leader may identify himself with the Nietzschean superman, and at the same time identify his own interests as those of the class, the nation or the race. It is further to be noticed that in the modern systems there is room only for a few such supermen, and they can only maintain their eminence through the willingness of their followers to lose themselves completely in the whole. Christianity, on the other hand, lays great stress upon the value of each individual person. While maintaining a proper respect for order and authority, it regards society as existing for the individual rather than the individual for society. In other words it rates the maxim 'all for each' as prior to the maxim 'each for all.'

This is but another way of saying that the characteristic attitude of the Christian is love for his neighbour: that is to say, not for humanity in general but for the precise individual with whom one comes in contact. Love in this sense is not primarily a matter of the emotions. It is not a question of liking or disliking, but of the set of the whole personality towards the service of others. Love in the Christian sense means the determined effort to bring about the highest good of all those with whom we come in contact. This is the real secret of Christian conduct. This is the rule by which every Christian must guide his life. It is not a question of occasional or spasmodic service. It does not mean giving ourselves in effort for those whom we like, while neglecting those whom we do not like. It is the steady determination to do the best that lies in our power for every individual we meet, whether friend or foe.

The difficulty of keeping such a rule is obvious, but Christian love is a supernatural grace. It is infused into us by God. It is Christ working in us by His Spirit.

Therefore the *amor hominis* must be preceded by the *amor dei*. It is never suggested that the Christian character can be maintained without the Christian faith. A generation ago it used to be said that while people disagreed about Christian dogma they all agreed about Christian conduct. Let us get rid of useless disputes about dogma, it was said, and we can give our undivided attention to insistence upon Christian conduct. Experience, however, has shown that if Christian belief is abandoned, Christian conduct soon disappears. The way of life for the Christian is the way of love. But that love could not be sustained were it not for the constant presence of the indwelling Christ.

6

Numerous attempts have been made to state the Christian code of conduct in a clear, concise and memorable form. The virtues have been enumerated as seven: four taken over from the old philosophic schools, namely prudence, temperance, justice and fortitude, and three from the New Testament, the theological virtues of faith, hope and love. The negative side of this teaching has been subsumed under the enumeration of the seven deadly sins: pride, anger, envy, gluttony, lust, covetousness, and sloth. The Roman Catholic Church has added to these lists the five precepts of the Church. '(1) On Sundays and other holy days of obligation to hear Mass and refrain from servile works. (2) On days appointed by the Church to fast and to abstain from flesh meat. (3) To confess our sins at least once a year. (4) To receive the Sacrament of the Holy Eucharist at least at Easter. (5) To recognize the necessities of the Church and her clergy.' The desire has often been expressed that there should be published some similar list of the duties expected of the laity in the Church of England. Recently this desire has found definite and insistent expression in the Church Assembly. Ultimately no doubt the Convocations will arrive at some form which they will issue with authority. In the meantime the Archbishops of Canterbury and York have put out a list of their own which has already commended itself to a large number of Church people.

All baptized and confirmed members of the Church must play their full part in its life and witness. That you may fulfil this duty, we call upon you:

> To follow the example of Christ in home and daily life, and to bear personal witness to Him.
> To be regular in private prayer day by day.
> To read the Bible carefully.
> To come to church every Sunday.
> To receive the Holy Communion faithfully and regularly.
> To give personal service to Church, neighbours and community.
> To give money for the work of parish and diocese, and for the work of the Church at home and overseas.

To this may be added as an explanatory note the rubric that occurs at the end of the Communion Service: 'Every parishioner shall communicate at least three times in the year, of which Easter to be one.'

7

In this connection questions are often asked about the Canons of the Church which are at present undergoing revision. It is well known that throughout the Middle Ages the law of the Church was expressed in certain Canons or rules, which were originally laws passed by the Œcumenical Councils but gradually grew by accretion into a vast body of regulations covering every detail of Church life. At the Reformation this law continued in force in England so far as it was not contrary to the Royal prerogative and the laws and customs of the realm. In addition to it the ecclesiastical law necessitated by the Reformation in this country was itself formed into a body of Canons which were passed by the Convocations in 1604. Since that time to the present day nothing of importance has been done to make clear how much of this ancient material is still in force, or to combine it into a coherent body of law. At the moment, however, the Convocations are busy compiling a new body of Canons with the intent of both revising and completing the Canons of 1604. In the meantime the Canons of 1604, with such amendments to them as have received Royal assent, are binding upon the laity and clergy in so far as they are declaratory of the ancient law and custom of the Church of England. It would, however, have altered the scope and purpose of this present book to have gone into details in a matter which is still *sub judice*. Sufficient, we may hope, has been said to make clear what is the mind of the Church of England upon the Christian rule of conduct.

CHAPTER X

THE GENIUS OF THE CHURCH OF ENGLAND

IN conclusion we must try to sum up what we have learned about the nature of religious authority and the way in which it is exercised in the Church of England.

I

The idea of authority is inherent in the very conception of a church. You cannot have a church without some kind of authority. We might go even further and say that you can have no religion without authority. Certainly this must be recognized by the Christian because as soon as he has begun to call Jesus Lord he has recognized the claim that Christ has upon his allegiance. This means that no man can do just what is right in his own eyes. It is true that where the Spirit of the Lord is there is liberty, but the Spirit is also the Spirit of order. As He brooded over the primæval chaos and moulded it into a compacted universe, so in the hearts of all God's people He works towards harmonious co-operation. 'Where two or three are gathered together in my name,' said our Lord, 'there am I in the midst of them.' His presence must involve a measure of unity. That unity will express itself in a common mind, and the common mind will always have a claim upon the consideration of each individual member.

Considerable harm has been done to this conception by the theory of an invisible church. There is a sense, of course, in which it is true that God's own are known only to Himself. The scribes and Pharisees sit in Moses' seat, but that does not mean that others will not enter into the Kingdom of Heaven before them. Nevertheless, sitting where they do, they have a certain authority and that authority must be recognized. That was the rule laid down by our Lord before His own Church replaced that of the Jews. 'Thus it becometh us to fulfil all righteousness.' The idea of an invisible church as the only kind of church founded by Christ has been generally abandoned by theologians. In spite of the divisions in Christendom it is generally agreed that our Lord's intention was to found one church and that a visible church. Of necessity this involves the notions both of unity and of authority. Because in modern times the external unity has been broken, the authority has inevitably been enfeebled; but within its own limits each body claiming to be a church exercises its own authority, without which indeed it would cease to exist.

There is no real conflict between authority and freedom. The individual only finds his true self in society. His character can only develop its proper powers in the company of his fellows. He fulfils himself in accepting authority. To put it another way, religious authority is not a force that binds us from without. God is not only within the Church, but within the individual soul. The authority of the Church is therefore not external only, but also internal. The law of God is written within men's hearts. They vibrate to the chord that is struck in eternity. This can be seen when we consider the special case of the authority of the Scriptures. God has revealed Himself in His Word and that is an authoritative revelation. It does not, however, exercise practical authority upon us as individuals unless and until there is a response to it in our own hearts. So the authority of the Church is not exercised upon unwilling souls but only upon those who know that as they yield to it they will find true liberty. God's service is perfect freedom. To be His slave is to reign as a king.

2

Such authority as belongs to the Church of England it claims to exercise as part of the Great Church. It does not function in isolation. It is itself the Mother Church of a world-wide Anglican Communion, or perhaps it would be truer to say that it is a sister church in a family of churches extending over the greater part of the world. Its bishops meet from time to time in solemn conclave with the bishops from its sister churches. It possesses the prestige of a body whose polity has been tried out in many lands, among different kinds of people, and under varied political systems.

Further, it must be noticed that although the unity of the Great Church has been broken, and there are many Christian bodies with which the Church of England is not in communion, it is nevertheless not a small isolated group of nationals living in an enclave of its own. It has a vital interest in other Christian denominations and they show an increasing interest in it. A number of metaphorical terms have been used to describe the special relationship of the Church of England to other churches not of its communion. It has sometimes been called a branch church and sometimes a bridge church, and its special theological position has been described as *via media*.

For the purpose of the discussion upon which we have entered such terms can be left on one side. What is important in the present connection is that the Church of England claims to be a miniature of the whole age-long and world-wide Church of God. Whatever is true of the whole Church is true of the Church of England. Those who love her will be forgiven for believing that with all her faults she represents the Church of the New Testament at least as faithfully as any other body of Christians. We believe that the promises made to the Church of the Apostolic Age will be fulfilled in her. She is part of the covenanted way of salvation and she receives the pledged grace of God.

To this position in relation to the whole of Christendom must be added the peculiar privileges she enjoys in her own country. She is a national Church, the Church of the English people; and she is an Established Church, the Church officially recognized by the State to represent religion within the boundaries of the country. It is admitted with sorrow that there are large bodies of Christians within the national boundaries who do not recognize her authority, although even of them many are willing to accept her leadership. Efforts have been made in the past to reconcile those who have departed from her, but it is fully recognized that she herself must bear some measure of blame for the historical divisions. Hitherto attempts to heal those divisions have been for the most part abortive, but to-day they are being renewed with fresh strength. There is, at the moment, a far greater measure of co-operation between the various sections of Christianity than there has ever been since the divisions were first made. Until we have been able to find some way of re-establishing our external unity, the Church of England claims authority only over her own members, but from them she does expect recognition of her claims and that measure of glad obedience which faithful membership of any society necessarily involves.

3

It follows from all this that the Church of England has its own special ethos. It is, as we have already seen, at once Catholic and Evangelical, recognizing no essential contradiction between these two aspects of Christian faith and practice. They are not mutually exclusive but complementary. If the two schools of thought have tended to express themselves in different types of worship even within the borders of the one organization, it has been by way of special emphasis upon one or other of the common factors that are inherent in our constitution. It may be that in recent developments the synthesis which seemed once to have been adequately expressed in the Anglicanism of the early post-Reformation period has been partially resolved again into its constituent elements. If this is so, we may believe that it is merely for a time, and that it has been providentially guided in order that each of these elements may receive fuller development and ultimately find unity again in a fresh synthesis at a higher level. In any case the essential unity still remains and still binds together those who are inclined to emphasize contrasted aspects of the common faith. Sometimes even in the same church building different services may express the views and tastes of different sections of the congregation, but all alike value membership of the same parochial family and work together for the same end. As the Church realizes that it lives and functions in the midst of a largely apathetic generation and recognizes that its fundamental task is still to carry on the work of its Master in proclaiming the Gospel to the unconverted, it may find in the prosecution of this common task a new incentive to unity not only of heart and mind, but also of doctrinal emphasis and liturgical taste. In the meantime it may be affirmed that the members of the Anglican Communion show a mutual consideration and a respect for individual freedom which are perhaps unique in Christendom and are certainly a valuable contribution to its total life.

This mutual accommodation may be found all the easier because of the traditional regard of the Church of England for sound learning. It is not suggested that every member is a keen theologian, far from it; but this Church has always from the earliest days of its separate existence shown a special reverence for scholarship. It has appreciated that scholarship all the more when not confined within narrow limits. Its leaders for the most part have been trained in the liberal tradition of classical and humanistic studies. The theologian has been expected not to limit his researches to narrow fields, but to display the relation of religion to life. In recent years far more attention than in the past has been paid to the technical training of the clergy in the theory and practice of their profession, but wider interests have never died out. Wherever possible a background of university studies has been secured for the ordinand before he enters upon the more restricted curriculum of the theological college. The result has been that a considerable proportion of the more scholarly clergy have been able to take their part in contributing through the liberal arts and sciences to the culture of the country.

It is, perhaps, natural that within this atmosphere freedom of thought and expression should be given special respect. The reason is not hard to understand. Those English Christians who at one time or another have separated from the National Church have been led inevitably to give a special and sometimes almost exclusive emphasis to their point of departure. They have naturally retained an exceptional interest in the practice or doctrine that then seemed all-important. Their range of interest has thus been narrowed. A similar result has been reached, though by a different route, in the Church of Rome. It has reserved for itself the right of promulgating from time to time new dogmas which become binding upon the faithful. For its members also the field of possible variation of opinion is thus progressively limited. In avoiding both these tendencies the Church of England is always inclined to reduce the necessary articles of faith to the fewest and simplest. It holds fast to the ancient creeds; and during the Reformation it issued its own confession in the shape of the Thirty-nine Articles. But those Articles were themselves of a mediating character rejecting extreme statements and nice definitions on either hand. Thus the door of opinion is left very wide open and authority is exercised in such a way as to restrict the limits of freedom as little as possible. In any case the Church of England admits of no doctrine as necessary to salvation which cannot be directly proved from the Scripture. This wide liberty of thought and practice is bound to lead from time to time to internal tension. Nevertheless with all its dangers it is still true to the spirit of the New Testament.

4

The constitution of the Church cannot be defined in the terms that are normally applied to political systems. It is neither an autocracy nor a democracy. It is essentially a theocracy. The Church believes itself to be under divine ordering. The intervention of Christ is shown not only in the revelation which He committed to it, but also in the apostolate which He founded. The Prayer Book states that the three orders of ministers belong to the

Apostolic Age, and it is implied that they are therefore in accordance with the mind of Christ. The Church of England believes that its own ministers are the direct successors of that early ministry. It attaches great importance to historical continuity because it believes that by this means can be guaranteed, as far as external proofs are concerned, the identity of the Church of to-day with the Church of the first generation. If it be asked why such importance should be attached to physical continuity, it can be answered that the Church partakes of a sacramental nature. There is an inward life of the Spirit which corresponds to sacramental grace, and there is the external organization which is parallel to the outward sign in every sacrament. Just as in any sacrament one must care for the outward sign because it is attached to the covenanted grace, so in the Church one must care for the succession of the ministry as the outward sign of continuous life.

To this extent therefore the Church is a theocracy, but the Church does not consist of the ministers only. It consists of the *laos*, the whole people of God. That means that the laity have their own indefeasible rights within it. This has always been the view of the Church of England. Normally it was expressed in the part that Crown and Parliament played in the government of Church affairs. In modern times, when it can no longer be held that the Church is co-terminous with the nation, and when Parliament contains a large proportion of non-Anglicans, some other opportunity has to be found of giving the faithful laity a chance of expressing their mind in ecclesiastical affairs. Consequently to-day we have not only the ancient Convocations to record the views of the bishops and clergy, but also the Church Assembly in which they are joined by elected members of the laity. This system is reflected in each diocese, where both clergy and laity meet with the bishop in the diocesan conference, and also in the parish, where the elected representatives of the laity meet with the incumbent on the parochial church council.

Thus what we have come to recognize in these days as democratic methods have been incorporated into the theocracy of the Church. They do not in themselves represent any new principle, but are merely modern ways of expressing the age-long recognition of God's relation to His whole Church. Thus in the exercise of authority the Church as a whole is engaged. The ministers have their own functions to perform, but that does not mean that they exercise any autocratic control of Church affairs. This applies even to the bishops who enjoy no autocratic powers but constitutional rights. When they act officially, they act only as representing the will and authority of the Church as a whole.

5

The way of life expected of the members is in such circumstances left as free as possible. Regulations and penalties are kept in the background. It is true that a communicant is bidden to make his Communion at least three times a year, but the main qualification for being placed on the electoral roll is a baptismal one. This inevitably means that more emphasis is placed on principles than on regulations. There is a wholesome fear of emphasizing the letter of the law while losing its spirit. This may be the reason why there is so large an outer fringe of non-practising members. However regrettable may be this incomplete recognition of the duties of membership, it still possesses one advantage. It means that the large proportion of the population still maintains a formal allegiance to the Church of England which might otherwise have been cut off from membership altogether. They are still on the side of the angels. One good result of the situation is that there is no sharp division in this country between a religious and an anti-religious section. The position here is thus quite different from that which prevails, for instance, in the United States of America and France.

At the same time it is obviously the duty of the Church to try to bring the lethargic and the apathetic multitudes to some acknowledgment of the claims of God. To fulfil such a purpose the Church in this country has a unique opportunity. It does not have to convert an antagonistic nation. It merely has to encourage all and sundry to act up to the profession which they already make. This task, of course, is hard enough, but at least these people have been baptized into Christ and the Church has a certain hold on them. It is probable that its influence can be exercised more readily by exhibiting a worthy way of life than by undue stress upon regimentation. If men can be brought to recognize that within the Church there is freedom and power, an opportunity of useful service and of growth into the fullness of manhood, they may ultimately recognize their privilege and may be brought to ally themselves wholeheartedly to the Christ who through these means has all along been seeking to win them to Himself.

6

It will be seen that the authority of the Church of England thus expressed offers no *absolute* security of salvation. If men desire security (as they should) the Church can assure them that Christ is the same yesterday, to-day and for ever. It cannot assure them with mathematical certainty that they will themselves exercise the grace of final perseverance. It can, however, give them the only kind of security that free men should want, namely, a moral security. It can assure them that through the means it has to offer grace is given. It is for them continually to use that grace and so walk the way of eternal life. The Church cannot guarantee that there will be a final solution to every difficulty and a complete answer to every question on this side of the grave, but it can and does announce that as people are faithful in their membership they will hear behind them at every moment of doubt and difficulty a voice saying, 'This is the Way, walk ye in it.'

Moreover the Church can offer them fellowship along the way. As in its services the priest, surrounded by his choir, with perhaps a layman reading the lesson, or attended by his servers at the altar together with a whole body of ministering laymen, typifies the unity of the whole family of God, so in every circumstance of life the person who accepts the authority of the Church finds himself one of a great company. Together they make their way through this world, enlightened as they go by the glory that streams from the throne of God and of the Lamb, pressing towards the final goal where awaits them that infinitude of bliss which God has stored up for those who love Him. Such people are the salt of the earth, the men who keep life pure and clean and sweet for the unthinking multitudes. They are the leaven that brings life to the whole lump. Caught up continually in the worship of the Church and carried to the Throne of Grace, they bring back to earth some of the glory and splendour they have witnessed there and radiate it throughout their human environment. Such men not only share the glad confidence of the redeemed in the salvation of their own souls, but carry on the Saviour's work of bringing release and stability to the world.